ELITE 203

World War II US Navy Special Warfare Units

EUGENE LIPTAK ILLUSTRATED BY JOHNNY SHUMATE
Series editor Martin Windrow

First published in Great Britain in 2014 by Osprey Publishing
PO Box 883, Oxford, OX1 9PL, UK
PO Box 3985, New York, NY 10185–3985, USA
E-mail: info@ospreypublishing.com

Osprey Publishing is part of the Osprey Group

© 2014 Osprey Publishing Ltd.

All rights reserved. Apart from any fair dealing for the purpose of private study, research, criticism or review, as permitted under the Copyright, Designs and Patents Act, 1988, no part of this publication may be reproduced, stored in a retrieval system, or transmitted in any form or by any means, electronic, electrical, chemical, mechanical, optical, photocopying, recording or otherwise, without the prior written permission of the copyright owner. Inquiries should be addressed to the Publishers.

A CIP catalog record for this book is available from the British Library

Print ISBN: 978 1 78096 053 1
PDF ebook ISBN: 978 1 78096 054 8
ePub ebook ISBN: 978 1 78096 055 5

Editor: Martin Windrow
Index by Alison Worthington
Typeset in Sabon and Myriad Pro
Originated by PDQ Media, Bungay, UK
Printed in China through Worldprint Ltd

14 15 16 17 18   10 9 8 7 6 5 4 3 2 1

Osprey Publishing is supporting the Woodland Trust, the UK's leading woodland conservation charity, by funding the dedication of trees.

www.ospreypublishing.com

DEDICATION
This book is respectfully dedicated to Father Roy Conry, O.Carm.

ACKNOWLEDGMENTS
The author expresses grateful appreciation to the following individuals and institutions for helping to make this book possible: James Barnes, Laurie Bryant, Robert Hanshew & Karin Haubold at the Naval History and Heritage Command; Roy Havekost of the US Navy Beach Jumpers Association; J.C. Johnson at the Howard Gotlieb Archival Research Center at Boston University, Boston, MA; Jim Madison of the UDT-SEAL Association; Dr Charles H. Miles; Sally Richards at the Imperial War Museum, London; Thomas Wheeler; the National Archives, College Park, MD; and Ruth McSween and the helpful staff at the National Navy UDT-SEAL Museum in Fort Pierce, Florida.

Abbreviations used in this text

APD	Transport, High Speed
ARB	Air-Sea Rescue Boat
BIS	Bureau of Investigation and Statistics (Chinese)
BJU	Beach Jumper Unit
BODP	Beach Obstacle Demolition Party
COPP	Combined Operations Pilotage Party (British)
LCC	Landing Craft, Control
LCI(D)	Landing Craft, Infantry, Demolition
LCI(G)	Landing Craft, Infantry, Gunboat
LCI(L)	Landing Craft, Infantry, Large
LCM	Landing Craft, Mechanized
LCN	Landing Craft, Navigation
LCP(R)	Landing Craft, Personnel, Ramp
LCR(S)	Landing Craft, Rubber, Small
LCS	Landing Craft, Support
LCT(A)	Landing Craft, Tank, Armored
LCVP	Landing Craft, Vehicle and Personnel
LST	Landing Ship, Tank
LVT	Landing Vehicle, Tracked
ML	Motor Launch (British)
MTB	Motor Torpedo Boat (British)
MU	Maritime Unit
NCDU	Naval Combat Demolition Unit
NDU	Naval Demolition Unit
OSS	Office of Strategic Services
POW	Prisoner of War
PT boat	Patrol Torpedo boat
SACO	Sino-American Cooperative Organization
UDT	Underwater Demolition Team
USAAF	United States Army Air Force
USN	United States Navy

CONTENTS

AMPHIBIOUS SCOUTS & RAIDERS   4
Origins • Weapons and equipment

Operations, Mediterranean and Europe: North Africa • Sicily • Italy • Adriatic Sea

• Normandy • Southern France

Operations, Pacific: Marshall Islands • New Guinea • New Britain • Philippines

BEACH JUMPERS   13
Origins • Weapons and equipment

Operations: Sicily • Italy • Southern France • Philippines

NAVAL COMBAT DEMOLITION UNITS   21
Forerunners: North Africa and Sicily • Establishment of NCDUs • Weapons and equipment

Operations, Pacific: Admiralty Islands • New Guinea • Philippines • Borneo

Operations, Europe: Omaha Beach • Utah Beach • Southern France

UNDERWATER DEMOLITION TEAMS   33
Origins • Weapons and equipment • Transportation: APDs and LCP(R)s

Operations: Marshall Islands • Saipan • Guam • Tinian • Peleliu • Philippines • Iwo Jima • Okinawa

• Borneo • Japanese surrender

NAVAL GROUP CHINA   50
Origins – Cdr Milton Miles • "Happy Valley" • Inter-service rivalries • Navy/Air Force cooperation

Operations: Guerrilla training and operations • Pact Doc • Weather stations • Coast-watching

• French Indochina • Japanese surrender

SELECT BIBLIOGRAPHY   63
INDEX   64

WORLD WAR II US NAVY SPECIAL WARFARE UNITS

AMPHIBIOUS SCOUTS & RAIDERS

With the Allies adopting the "Germany First" strategy, and the US Marines fully committed to the Pacific, the US Navy and US Army established a joint Amphibious Scouts & Raiders school at Little Creek, Virginia in July 1942, in preparation for amphibious operations in the European theater. The primary function of the Scouts & Raiders was to locate and mark beachheads to ensure that landing forces would find them easily, whereas the "Raider" portion of their training in small arms was primarily for self-defense.

US Army doctrine called for troops to be landed by night at high tide, so that there would be a shorter extent of exposed beach for soldiers to cross before they could find cover. The S&R recruits were therefore trained to locate the predetermined landing area in darkness, and then guide in the subsequent landing craft with signal lights. Scouts & Raiders were not organized into designated units, but operated in small teams wherever they were needed. In January 1943 the school moved to Fort Pierce, Florida, and that December it became the sole responsibility of the US Navy as the US Army began withdrawing its personnel from the program.

In early 1944, after it was determined that enough Scouts & Raiders had been trained for operations in Europe, the Amphibious Roger program was initiated to focus on training personnel for raiding operations in China. Only a handful of Scouts & Raiders saw action in China, while hundreds of them lingered in staging camps in India until the end of the war (see "Naval Group China/Inter-service rivalries", below.) In March 1945 the school was renamed the Amphibious Scout School; it was closed down in March 1946, after a total of 1,200 men had been trained as Scouts & Raiders.

Scouts & Raiders used kayaks throughout the Mediterranean theater for nighttime beach reconnaissance missions, finding them sturdy, inconspicuous, and easy to operate provided the water was not too rough. These two scouts are seen practicing with a kayak off Salerno, Italy. (National UDT-SEAL Museum)

Weapons & equipment
Scouts & Raiders used standard landing craft as scout boats, before they took command of LCC and LCS control boats later in the war. Some of the scout boats were armed with rocket-launchers to provide fire support. Infrared lights were used for clandestine signaling between craft, but early models burned out too quickly due to improper wiring. Field-expedient versions

Rubber boats, such as this LCR(S) of Underwater Demolition Team 7 off Peleliu, were used for special operations by the US Navy. Paddles were the most common form of propulsion, since outboard motors were both noisy and unreliable. (National UDT-SEAL Museum)

were made with infrared paper placed over the lenses of damage control lights, or clusters of five-cell flashlights; but infrared paper was fragile, and when it split over the lens it revealed slivers of bright light that attracted enemy fire. Blue, red, green, or yellow cellophane sheets were also taped to the lenses of damage control lights to designate the specific color-coded beach to which the scout boat was assigned. Battle lanterns equipped with their own colored lenses were later mounted on field-made swivel mounts along the gunwales. Hooded five-cell flashlights pointed out to sea were also used for signaling, but in certain atmospheric conditions enemy defenses could trace the beams they produced back to the scout boat.

For beach reconnaissance or other clandestine missions the Scouts & Raiders used the 250lb Landing Craft Rubber (Small); this was 12ft long, 5ft 11in wide, and held (at a pinch) up to seven men. Its sturdiness, portability, and lack of a radar profile made the LCR(S) ideal for irregular operations. Although it was fitted with brackets to accommodate outboard motors, their unreliability made paddles the standard method of propulsion. Inflation could be achieved with CO^2 bottles, hand pumps, or air lines from surface ships. Scouts & Raiders also used kayaks made of rubberized canvas wrapped around a plywood frame fitted together with light metal pipe. These were found to be easy to assemble, easy to paddle, quiet, and durable. In the dark they lacked a discernible silhouette on the water, and could get through the surf more easily and safely than a rubber boat when it was necessary to take a closer look at the beach. They performed well in calm waters, but were difficult to handle and fragile in rough seas. Stealth was their greatest ally, since they lacked the speed to make a quick getaway if discovered.

OPERATIONS: MEDITERRANEAN & EUROPE

North Africa
In the early hours of November 8, 1942, scout boats (each deploying from an attack transport) guided American landing craft in toward their designated beachheads near Safi, Fedala, and Mehdia on the Atlantic coast of western Morocco. With a crew of five Scouts & Raiders, each scout boat located the assigned beach in the dark by identifying key landmarks and silhouettes. Stationed offshore, the scout boats averted chaos and disaster by directing lost landing craft to the correct beaches with their signal lights.

Five Scouts & Raiders in a rubber boat from the submarine USS *Barb* were assigned to guide the destroyers USS *Cole* and USS *Bernadou* into Safi harbor so their onboard US Army detachments could seize its port facilities intact. After paddling for several hours the Scouts & Raiders discovered that they were further offshore than planned. They successfully reached the buoy at the approach to the harbor only to discover that it was too small to use. An attempt to signal the destroyers from a nearby breakwater was thwarted by a French sentry just as the assault began, compelling the Scouts & Raiders to leave. A scout boat from the transport USS *Harris* reached the northern end of the same breakwater and used its infrared lights and hooded flashlight to guide the destroyers into Safi harbor, and the soldiers captured it intact.

In the Mediterranean, rough seas off Algiers prevented the scout boat from the amphibious assault ship USS *Leedstown* from guiding in the landing craft, but it rescued others that had run out of fuel. Shortly afterward the *Leedstown* was crippled by a torpedo from a Luftwaffe attack, and was sunk the next day by another torpedo from a U-boat. All the Scouts & Raiders aboard the USS *Leedstown* survived.

Sicily

In the spring of 1943 a team of five Scouts & Raiders conducted reconnaissance of Sicilian beaches along with British Combined Operations Pilotage Party (COPP) teams in two-man kayaks, operating from Royal Navy submarines based in Malta. In June, the Scouts & Raiders trained 50 US Army volunteers along the Tunisian coast in preparation for the invasion of Sicily. In the early hours of July 10, 1943, LCS scout boats launched from offshore LSTs were each directed toward their assigned American beachheads by reference vessels stationed a mile offshore in the Gulf of Gela. Due to rough weather and delayed arrivals to the beachhead, some scout boats were unable to deploy their kayaks to help mark the flanks of the landing beaches as planned, but they were able to position themselves in the middle of the beach to guide in the landing craft with their signal lights. One kayak crew was able to place lights on the flanks of Yellow Beach, although attracting machine-gun fire after one man landed in front of a manned pillbox; he then sat directly underneath its embrasure to shine his hooded flashlight seaward. The Scouts & Raiders were able to accomplish their mission despite sporadic interference from searchlights, shore batteries, and machine guns, to which the scout boats replied with 4.5in rockets and .50cal machine-gun fire. With the American troops ashore, Sicily became the last operation where US Army personnel served in the ranks of the Scouts & Raiders.

A

SCOUTS & RAIDERS

1: Scout boat captain, Morocco, November 1942
During Operation "Torch" landing craft used as scout boats were armed with rockets to provide close fire support to the landings along the Moroccan coast. In the event, the lack of serious resistance on the beaches that contributed to the overall success of the landings precluded the need for the boats to fire their rockets. This captain of a scout boat wears a blue sweater over his khaki uniform, and, anticipating the use of rockets, an M1 helmet over a protective flash-proof hood.

2: Kayak crewman, Mediterranean, summer 1943
A group of Scouts & Raiders operated kayaks at night to conduct beach reconnaissance on the shores of Sicily, Italy, and Normandy. The black-dyed herringbone twill (HBT) coveralls worn during training at Fort Pierce were adopted for these types of operations, and faces and hands were blacked with greasepaint for nighttime reconnaissance missions. This scout is holding a wooden paddle used to propel the kayak; maps, binoculars, extra water, and emergency rations were also carried.

3: LCC captain, Southern France, August 1944
Many Scouts & Raiders found themselves spread out amongst the fleet, where they applied their training in beach conditions and landmark recognition in an advisory role as part of ships' crews or naval staff. Some captained scout boats that guided in landing craft during the Normandy and southern France invasions in the summer of 1944. This officer blends in with the rest of the crew of his Landing Craft Control, wearing a kapok life vest over his khakis.

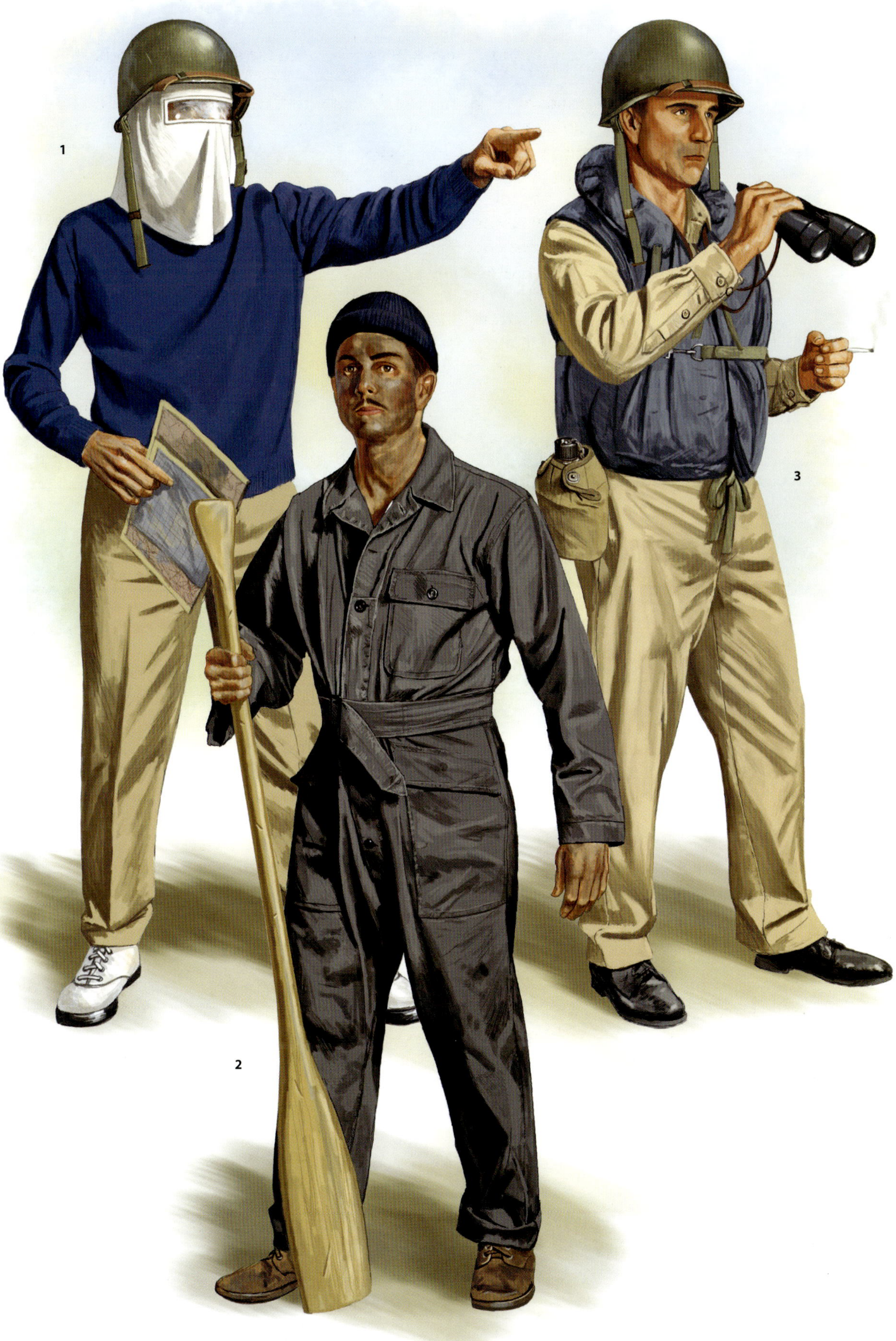
1
2
3

Italy

In the early morning hours of September 9, 1943, reference vessels were positioned several miles off Salerno to guide in the Scouts & Raiders tasked with surveying the four designated landing beaches just ahead of the Allied task force. Off each beach two Scouts & Raiders departed their LCS scout boat in a kayak to conduct a reconnaissance of the landing areas. Despite the dark and the mountainous terrain, the kayak crews were able to locate both beach exits and shore batteries that had revealed themselves by counterbattery fire against the Allied bombardment. At the end of their clandestine survey, each kayak signaled to its scout boat the position it was to take to guide the incoming landing craft to its respective beach. Despite being caught in the crossfire between Allied ships and enemy coastal defenses the Scouts & Raiders returned to their scout boats unscathed, although shrapnel from an 88mm shell-burst hit one kayak. The scout boats were successful in directing the landing craft to their correct beaches despite the damage they sustained while evading German artillery fire.

Later that year, with the Allied advance stalled along the German "Gustav Line," an amphibious landing to flank the defensive line was planned. Just before midnight on December 30, 1943, three Scouts & Raiders along with three British scouts in three two-man kayaks were dropped off the coast at Anzio by PT-201 to check for any sandbars or shoals that might impede the planned invasion. The nighttime survey was successful, but two Scouts & Raiders in one kayak were declared missing in action after failing to return to the PT boat. Star shells and small-arms fire were observed and heard respectively in the area to which they were assigned, but their exact fate remains a mystery.

Early in the morning of January 22, 1944, scout boats left their LSTs to use their colored lights to guide in the landing craft toward Anzio. One kayak from a scout boat paddled close to Yellow Beach to use its battle lantern to guide in the landing by US Army Rangers. In a "friendly-fire" incident PT-201 was hit by gunfire from the minesweeper USS *Sway* that narrowly missed US Fifth Army commander Gen Mark Clark, but killed a Scout & Raider officer who had just returned from a mission off the Anzio beachhead.

Seen here on the island of Vis in June 1944, these Scouts & Raiders scouted beaches ahead of Allied commando raids throughout the Adriatic, and helped rescue downed Allied airmen who reached the Yugoslavian coast. Except for dress uniforms for official occasions, personnel in all the special units described in this book wore a mixture of practical uniform items in the field, including Navy chambray shirts and dungarees, Army fatigues, and HBT coveralls. (National UDT-SEAL Museum)

Adriatic Sea

In May 1944, two teams of Scouts & Raiders, along with Beach Jumper Unit 4 (see below) with four Air-Sea Rescue Boats, became the US Navy Adriatic Special Operations Group on the island of Vis off the coast of Yugoslavia. The ARBs rescued Allied pilots forced down in the Adriatic; and they deposited Scouts & Raiders in rubber boats along the Yugoslavian coast to pick up both airmen and agents, and to survey landing areas for potential commando raids. ARBs also delivered supplies to Tito's communist Partisans on the mainland.

On the night of May 10, two Scouts & Raiders with signal lights paddled from an ARB to a beach on the island of Sota to usher in a raiding force of British Commandos, an OSS Greek Operational Group, and Partisans. A team of 15 men from BJU-4 also landed with a rocket-launcher and a load of 4.5in rockets to provide fire support for the operation, which resulted in the island being seized and the garrison neutralized. The Adriatic Special Operations Group supported subsequent raids against other nearby islands and along the mainland coast. BJU-4 also transmitted demands for surrender to German garrisons on these islands. In July, BJU-4 conducted a deception operation while supporting a Commando raid on the coast straddling the border between Albania and Yugoslavia. This effort inadvertently led the Germans to believe that they were under air attack, provoking a barrage of anti-aircraft fire.

Soon afterward the Adriatic Special Operations Group began to disband, with the Scouts & Raiders rejoining their comrades at Salerno for the invasion of southern France, and BJU-4 leaving for its base at Ocracoke, North Carolina in September 1944.

Normandy

In preparation for the cross-Channel invasion, British COPP teams from the Isle of Wight conducted clandestine nighttime surveys of certain beaches along the Normandy coast to determine their suitability for amphibious landings. On one moonless night in February 1944, two Scouts & Raiders accompanied the COPPs in LCNs towed by Royal Navy MTBs to a point 8 miles off Omaha Beach. They gathered sand samples for analysis to see if the beach could withstand the weight of the tanks and other vehicles that were to cross it. Soundings were also taken every 20 yards to within 150 yards of the shore, until one LCN accidentally ran aground, alerting the Germans. Despite the resultant machine-gun fire the LCNs withdrew safely with the entire survey party back to their MTBs. The two Scouts & Raiders would later return in a kayak, from which they swam ashore to gather more sand samples without being detected.

On D-Day itself, Scouts & Raiders aboard LCCs and LCSs guided the first waves in toward Omaha Beach. The confusion caused by the smoke from the preliminary bombardment, heavy fire from the German defenses, and the strong current offshore caused many landing craft to miss their assigned sectors. The scout boats provided whatever fire support they could with 4.5in rockets and .50cal machine guns; one German machine-gun nest in a second-story window was wiped out with a rocket from a scout boat. Scout boats also conducted traffic control to and from the beach, pulled infantrymen from the water, rescued crewmen from sinking vessels, and helped evacuate casualties to ships offshore.

Three miles off Utah Beach lay the Îles de Saint-Marcouf, where it was believed the Germans had set up coastal artillery and observation posts on the Île du Large. Scouts & Raiders trained a detachment of US Army cavalrymen assigned to capture the island in rubber-boat handling. Guided in by an LCS, the Scouts & Raiders led the cavalrymen ashore, only to discover that the island was unoccupied, unfortified, but booby-trapped with land mines that soon inflicted several casualties. Off Utah Beach itself, LCC-60, with a former Scout & Raider officer aboard, discovered that nearby Uncle Red Beach was devoid of control vessels to guide the incoming first wave. LCC-60 was successful in single-handedly directing the landing craft toward that beach as well as its assigned Tare Green Beach. Confusion and delayed timetables saw the landing craft heading for Uncle Red Beach divert around a row of swimming Duplex Drive tanks to avoid swamping them, thus landing 500 yards to the left of their assigned beach.

When the Normandy beachheads had been secured, Scouts & Raiders surveyed small harbors, and took soundings and marked off the areas where the artificial Mulberry harbors were to be assembled.

Southern France

On the night of June 16, 1944, a Scouts & Raiders officer from the APD USS *Tattnall* guided in French Commandos in rubber boats who landed and occupied the island of Pianosa, while French forces liberated the island of Elba further north.

This pontoon boat was one of three made with salvaged parts from French seaplanes; 22ft long, they held two men and could achieve 30 knots. During tests of their seaworthiness one exploded and a second sank, but the sole survivor was successfully used during Operation "Dragoon" on the French Mediterranean coast. (National UDT-SEAL Museum)

B

ADRIATIC & MEDITERRANEAN, SPRING-SUMMER 1944

1 & 2: Adriatic Special Operations Group, Vis island, spring 1944

As part of the Allied effort in the spring of 1944 to support Josef Tito's Partisans from a base on the island of Vis, located 31 miles off the coast of Yugoslavia, two teams of Scouts & Raiders and Beach Jumper Unit 4 formed the US Navy Adriatic Special Operations Group. With little opportunity to conduct deception operations, the Beach Jumpers in their ARBs supported commando raids, the rescue of downed aircrew, and agent recovery, while the Scouts & Raiders surveyed the beaches along the coast and neighboring islands ahead of these operations. These two men wear a typical range of field clothing. The Scout & Raider maintains his naval identity with his "dixie cap" while wearing US Army coveralls, and has a .45cal M1911A1 semiautomatic holstered on his pistol belt. The Beach Jumper wears a US Army "M1941" Parsons field jacket with his US Navy dungaree trousers, and is armed with a UD42 Marlin submachine gun in 9mm Parabellum caliber.

3: NCDU-54, St Tropez harbor, August 1944

Clearing harbors of mines and sunken ships was a task undertaken by Naval Combat Demolition Units (see later chapter) to allow Allied supply ships to enter captured ports. The self-contained Jack Browne rebreather unit was used for operating underwater in shallow areas. About to dive into St Tropez harbor in southern France, this demolitioneer wears a belt of lead weights to maintain slight negative buoyancy while submerged. The rope around his waist serves as his safety line. He holds a satchel charge that will be placed next to an obstruction and detonated electrically from the surface.

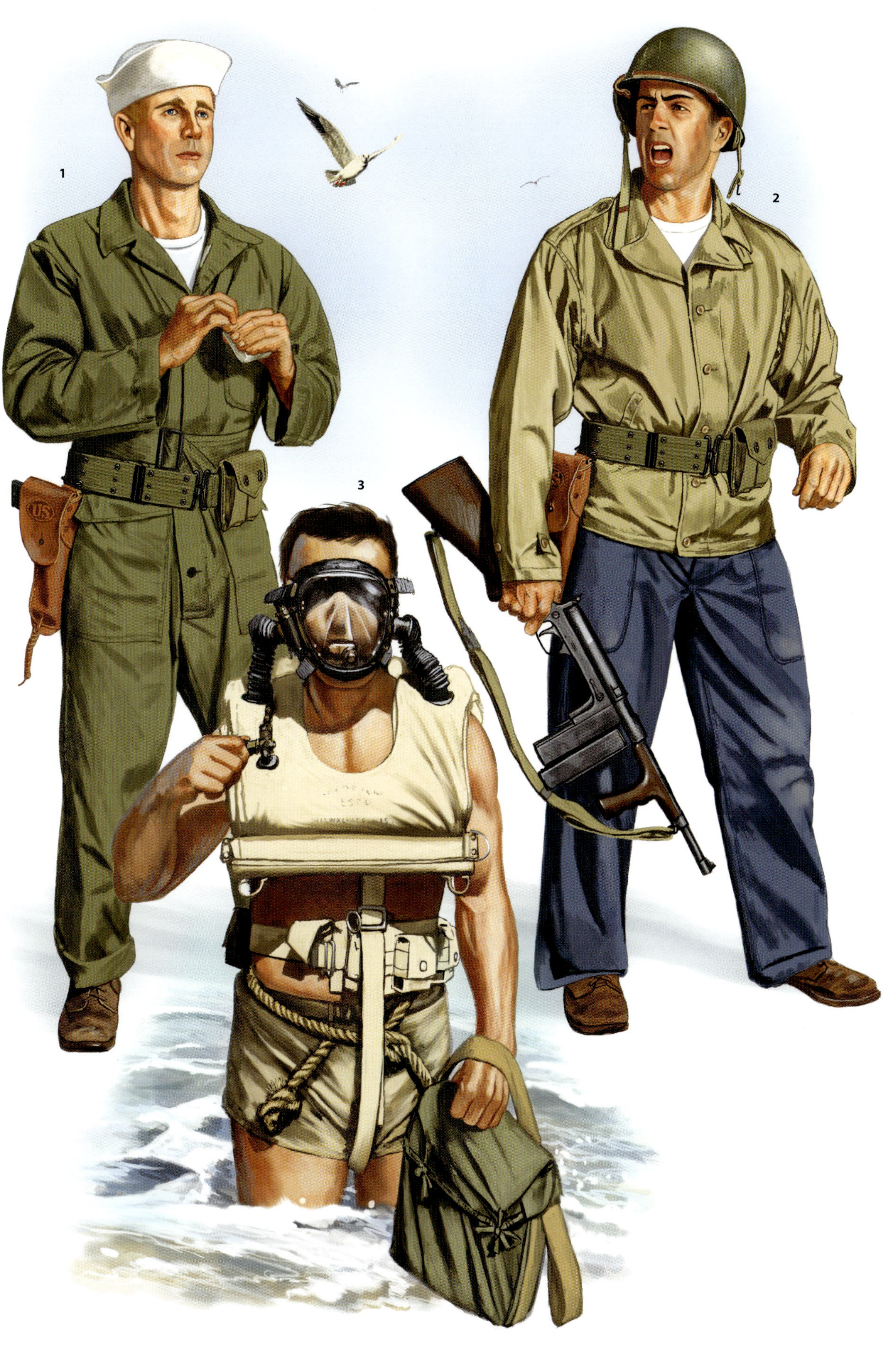
1
2
3

The invasion of southern France (Operation "Dragoon") began in the early hours of August 15, when Scouts & Raiders from the USS *Tattnall* conducted a reconnaissance of the beaches on the islands of Port-Cros and Île du Levant in rubber boats ahead of the 1st Special Service Force, who soon captured the islands. Scouts & Raiders also guided French Commandos ashore to the south at Cap Negre and at Théoule-sur-Mer to the north to secure both flanks of the landing area. Scout boats, along with a field-made motorized pontoon boat, located key landmarks that delineated Blue and Yellow Beaches in the Delta sector. They searched for but did not locate any offshore obstacles, before placing a buoy in the water to mark the approach for the incoming landing craft. Scout boats also provided covering fire with rockets and machine guns until the beachheads were secured.

OPERATIONS: PACIFIC

One team of Scouts & Raiders successfully scouted the landing beaches in the Marshall Islands alongside Underwater Demolition Teams 1 & 2 (see below) in January 1944. When the mission of scouting beaches was given to the UDTs, some Scouts & Raiders served aboard attack transports as intelligence officers and boat-handlers, while the majority of them volunteered for the UDTs.

A few later served as replacements for an amphibious scout unit in the southwest Pacific that was initially composed of volunteers from all the services of the US and Australian military, plus natives from New Guinea and New Britain. What became known as Seventh Amphibious Force Special Service Unit 1 began training at Cairns on the northeast coast of Australia in July 1943, before moving the following month to Fergusson Island off the eastern coast of New Guinea, to scout potential beachheads as the vanguard of Gen Douglas MacArthur's leapfrogging campaign toward the Philippines. From September through December 1943, teams were sent by PT boat to explore potential landing sites at Finschhafen in New Guinea, along with Cape Bushing, Gasmata, Cape Gloucester and Arawe in New Britain.

In late 1943 US Navy personnel who served in the US/Australian Special Service Unit 1 formed by Seventh Amphibious Force surveyed potential landing beaches and gathered other hydrographic intelligence on the coasts of New Guinea and New Britain, while other teammates scouted the approaches off the beach. These men are on a jungle training exercise between operations. (National UDT-SEAL Museum)

With their rubber boats hidden along the shore, teams gathered beach soundings and hydrographic data, surveyed areas for potential airfields, and pinpointed Japanese defenses for several days at a time, while avoiding all contact with the Japanese and local natives. Members from SSU-1 served in the beach parties that supported the landing by the Marines on Cape Gloucester in late December 1943.

By late November 1943, SSU-1 had in fact been renamed the Seventh Amphibious Force Scouts as the Australians withdrew their personnel and the US Army formed the Alamo Scouts. When they were not conducting scouting missions behind enemy lines, personnel from the Seventh Amphibious Force Scouts served in beach parties during amphibious assaults in New Guinea and the Philippines. On June 25, 1944 the US Navy submarine S-47 dropped off a team accompanied by several Alamo Scouts to survey the beaches at Sansapor in western New Guinea for several weeks. They accomplished their mission undetected, despite the presence of several Japanese barges in the area.

On the night of October 18, two teams of Seventh Amphibious Force Scouts, each accompanied by 100 men from the 6th Ranger Bn, installed beacon lights on the islands of Dinagat and Homonhon in the Surigao Strait, to guide the US Seventh Fleet into Leyte Gulf. On March 9, 1945, one team surveyed the landing beach near Zamboanga in southern Mindanao despite Japanese machine-gun and sniper fire, while another team conducted a brief survey of the beach near Floillo on southeastern Panay. In April, a scout team successfully surveyed beaches along Davao Gulf in Mindanao despite continuous machine-gun fire from inshore caves. The last wartime operation of the Seventh Amphibious Force Scouts was a hydrographic survey of the beaches at Brunei Bay in Borneo on June 8, 1945 ahead of the Australian landing there.

Seen here aboard the destroyer USS *Endicott* in August 1944, LtCdr Douglas Fairbanks Jr (left, wearing dark blue deck jacket with white "U.S. NAVY" shoulder title) played a key role in the formation of the Beach Jumpers. Captain Henry Johnson (center) commanded Special Operations Task Group 80.4 during Operation "Dragoon," and LtCdr John Bulkeley (right) captained the USS *Endicott*, which helped to sink two German corvettes during the South of France invasion. Earlier that year Bulkeley had commanded a small detachment of PT boats that conducted covert operations in the English Channel and participated on D-Day. He was a recipient of the Medal of Honor for his actions while leading PT boats in the Philippines, which included rescuing Gen MacArthur from Corregidor in March 1942. (Douglas Fairbanks Jr Collection, Howard Gotlieb Archival Research Center, Boston University)

BEACH JUMPERS

In July 1942 the head of British Combined Operations, Adm Lord Louis Mountbatten, invited his longtime friend Douglas Fairbanks Jr to join his command to observe their methods and operations so as to pass along the lessons they were learning to the Americans. A popular Hollywood actor, and a lieutenant (junior grade) in the US Naval Reserve since April 1941, Fairbanks was already a veteran of several Atlantic convoys. The invitation allowed him to become familiar with the conduct of amphibious commando raids, and he grasped the usefulness of employing deception to mislead enemy forces during such assaults. After participating in several cross-Channel raids, Fairbanks was asked by Mountbatten to return home and make the case for the US Navy to form its own tactical deception unit for use in amphibious operations.

In fact, by the time Fairbanks presented this idea to Adm Henry K. Hewitt (commander of US Naval Forces, Northwest Africa Waters) in January 1943, the US Navy

13

had already been convinced of the merits of such a unit due to the efforts of Prof Harold Burris-Meyer of the Stevens Institute of Technology. An expert in the effective use of sound in theatrical productions, Burris-Meyer was in charge of research and development for the National Defense Research Committee's Project 17:3-1, which tested concepts of using sound to harm, terrify, and deceive the enemy. Burris-Meyer himself developed a prototype sonic deception device, called a Heater, which projected the simulated sound of an impending amphibious assault upon a targeted shoreline. An exercise on the night of October 27, 1942 off Sandy Hook, New Jersey vindicated his efforts; the defenders were lured to the south end of the beach by the sound of an approaching assault force, while the actual landing at its northern end went in unhindered.

The naval deception unit known as the Beach Jumpers was formally established at Camp Bradford, Virginia in March 1943; it would eventually have 70 officers and 400 sailors in nine numbered units. Lacking sufficient rank to be given command, Lt Fairbanks was placed in charge of recruitment, training, and supply, along with the planning and supervision of operations. Burris-Meyer became a lieutenant commander in the US Navy to assist with sonic equipment training, while Project 17:3-1 refocused its efforts to develop equipment solely for the Beach Jumpers. That December they were transferred to Ocracoke, North Carolina, where they continued to learn how to convincingly simulate an invasion force with sound projection, radar-jamming, rocket barrages, and false voice and coded radio traffic.

Weapons & equipment

Beach Jumpers primarily used fast 63ft Air-Sea Rescue Boats to conduct their deception operations along enemy coastlines, and personnel were cross-trained to handle any of the crew functions if necessary. Smoke-generators were installed to produce smokescreens, while smoke pots mounted on the sides and stern of the ARBs or tossed into the water helped prolong the smokescreens. Standard 4.5in rockets from launchers placed near the bow were fired to simulate preliminary naval bombardments, while the ARB's two twin .50cal machine guns, and TNT charges with delay fuses randomly thrown overboard, added to the effect. Roman candles attached to wooden X-shaped floats were also placed in the water to mimic 20mm fire. Another interesting innovation developed by the Beach Jumpers were inflatable

---

C

BEACH JUMPERS

1: Sentry, BJU-1; Capri, Italy, September 1943
After occupying the island of Capri as part of Task Group 80.4, BJU-1 used it as a base during the capture of neighboring islands in the Gulf of Naples. Despite their primary role of seaborne deception, the Beach Jumpers in their ARBs were often involved with commando operations and intelligence-gathering. The pleasant Mediterranean climate is allowing this Beach Jumper to pull sentry duty with only his standard US Navy chambray shirt, dungaree trousers, and pith helmet; he carries an M1903 Springfield bolt-action rifle.

2: ARB crewman, BJU-3; Calvi, Corsica, August 1944
This Air-Sea Rescue Boat crewman is preparing to load a high-explosive 4.5in rocket into its launcher for the deception operations that supported the Allied "Dragoon" landings in southern France. These launchers provided the punch to the deception that an amphibious landing was about to take place. "Chaff" was also loaded into the nosecones of 3.5in rockets, which exploded to spread aluminum clouds in front of the beachhead to deceive enemy radar. Two of these launchers mounted on the bow of the ARB were fired remotely from a control box located on the bridge.

3: Lieutenant, BJU-2; Camp Bradford, Virginia, May 1943
This US Navy lieutenant is about to ignite a smoke pot for training purposes. The 32lb of smoke compound was used to produce smokescreens to veil the true composition of Beach Jumper units during their deception operations offshore. A group of them were located on the stern of ARBs, while others were made buoyant and tossed into the water to maintain the smokescreens after the ARBs had left. A pull tab on the top of the smoke pot revealed its igniter button, which was struck with an accompanying ignition match.

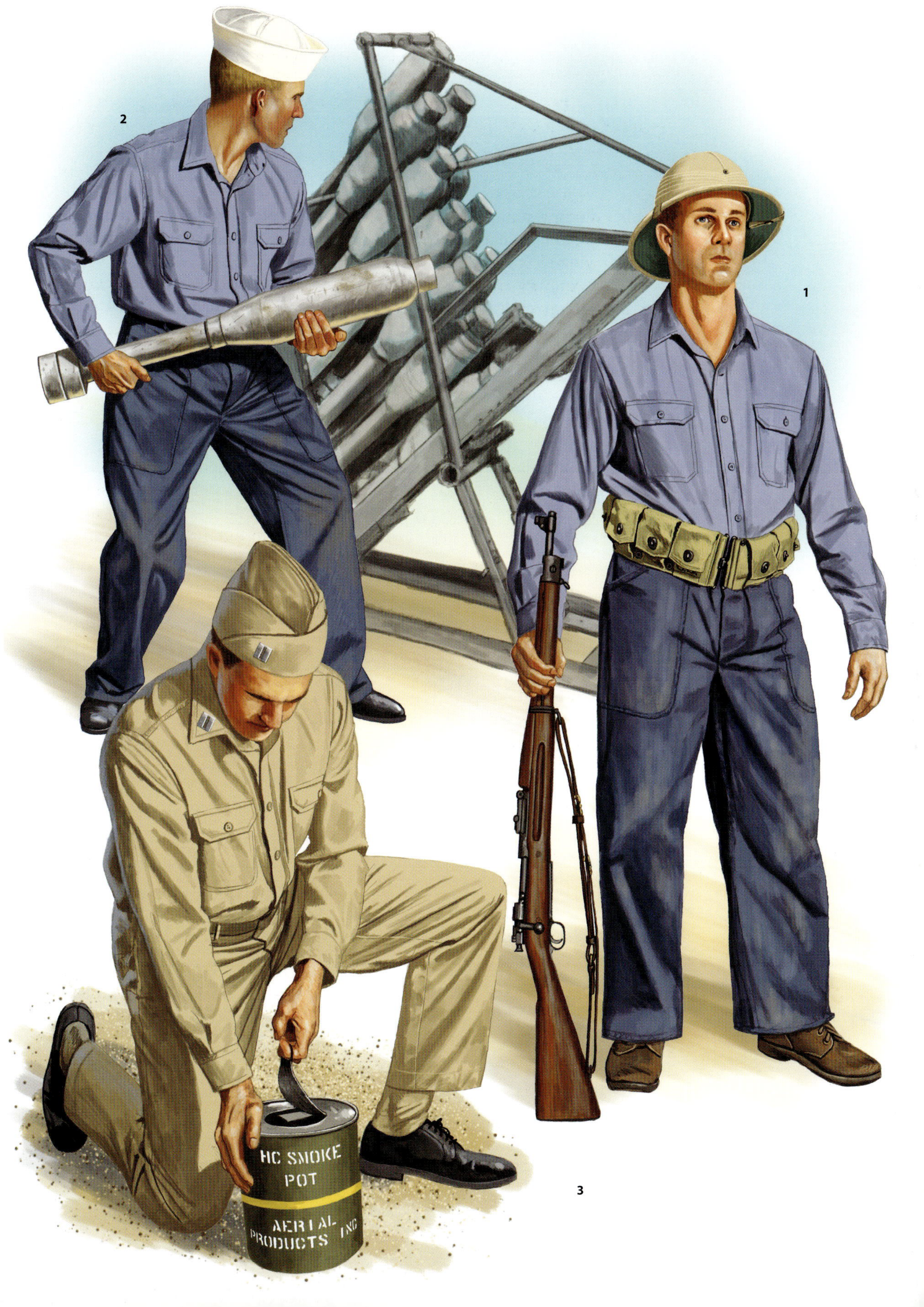
2
1
3
HC SMOKE
POT
AERIAL
PRODUCTS INC

LEFT
This 63ft Air-Sea Rescue Boat from BJU-1 is seen off the coast of southern France during Operation "Dragoon" in August 1944. Under magnification it can be seen to have two rocket-launchers on the bow, and a row of smoke pots along the starboard side forward. Although ARBs were used for almost all of their operations during the war, the Beach Jumpers preferred the faster and better-armed PT boats. (Paul E. Burkey Collection, US Navy Beach Jumpers Association)

RIGHT
Here an ARB carries a naval balloon on its stern. Foil strips would hang down from the balloon while it was towed at least 300 yards behind the ARB during deception operations, to make the radar reflection of the ARB appear larger on enemy radarscopes. (Paul E. Burkey Collection, US Navy Beach Jumpers Association)

rubber dummy soldiers weighted down at the bottom to keep them upright in the surf; in poor nighttime visibility their bobbing made it appear that they were "trying to wade ashore."

Beach Jumper equipment was portable and could be installed aboard other small naval craft that were available in theater, such as PT boats and landing craft. Trihedral or box kite-shaped multitrihedral corner reflectors and pairs of chicken-wire rectangles that bounced back radar waves were attached to Beach Jumper craft to make them appear bigger on radarscopes. This effect was enhanced with naval balloons that were towed 300–800 yards behind the ARBs with 13ft x 2in-wide foil strips attached to them. The ARBs could sail at up to 30 knots without causing the balloons to gyrate uncontrollably.

Radar-jamming sets were installed aboard Beach Jumper craft to fool enemy coastal radar stations into thinking that an actual landing was taking place by jamming their frequencies. A radar station operating undisturbed on a specific frequency will display an echo from an approaching ship as a vertical spike on its screen; when a radar set is being jammed the radarscope displays innumerable spikes, rendering it ineffective. This was accomplished with a radar jammer tuned to any frequency emitting from a radar station; the radar wavelengths would be drowned out with random signals that sounded like radio static. Jamming sets used by the Beach Jumpers included the APQ-2 Rug, APT-2 Carpet, and the APT-3 Mandrel, to counter the

In this still from an OSS Field Photographic training film, two inflatable rubber dummies are bobbing in the ocean off Camp Bradford, VA during a training exercise in May 1943. They were dropped overboard during the pre-dawn confusion of a deception operation to simulate soldiers wading toward shore, and were first used in action on June 17, 1944 during the liberation of the Mediterranean island of Elba. (Author's photograph)

The Heater sonic projector had a magnetic wire recorder that transmitted sounds of an amphibious landing, to include anchor chains being dropped into the water, landing craft motoring toward shore, and tanks clanking up onto the beach. These sounds were previously recorded during training exercises and naval maneuvers. (Author's photograph)

German Seetakt, Würzburg, and Freya radars respectively. The jamming sets were often used with an APR-1 intercept receiver that allowed an operator to detect enemy radar waves while listening for their unique signals through earphones. The Beach Jumpers either performed "barrage" jamming with multiple sets to disrupt a wide range of frequencies in a given area, or "spot" jamming which affected specified frequencies from specific radar stations. The exact frequency of a radar station needed to be determined beforehand so the jamming sets could be adjusted accordingly, to avoid any gaps in the jamming effort that might compromise the entire deception.

The Moonshine set was designed by the British as an alternative to jamming by making German radar operators believe they had detected a larger body of ships or aircraft than were actually present. Activating automatically when it detected the pulses emitting from Freya early-warning radar, Moonshine produced a greater number of spikes on German

Heater sonic projectors are seen here in waterproof cases aboard a landing craft at Camp Bradford. The effectiveness of these sonic projectors was determined by the wind conditions along the enemy-held coast. Calm or offshore winds obliged the Beach Jumpers to come closer inshore, while onshore winds allowed them to operate effectively further out. (Author's photograph)

radarscopes than those already reflecting off the Beach Jumper craft. One set could cover only one specific frequency at a time, so several sets were needed on a given operation if multiple frequencies were to be expected. Since they only operated at periodic intervals by night, the Beach Jumpers were able to use Moonshine effectively while using the darkness to cloak the true size of their force. Another radar-deception measure was tiny radar-reflective foil strips ("chaff"; called "window" by the Royal Air Force) packed into the nosecones of 3.5in rockets that exploded in front of the beachhead. One nosecone contained up to 76,800 strips, each cut 3/16in wide and varying in length from 1½in up to 16in, to jam the different frequencies transmitted by German radar. Several bursts of chaff could simulate the radar reflections of an entire amphibious assault. Its disadvantage was that as the clouds of foil floated down the reflections they presented appeared to be standing still, not moving forward like an actual fleet.

The physics of sound projection precluded the simple approach of recording the sounds of approaching landing craft and broadcasting them toward an enemy coastline. What is being transmitted from a ship may not be heard as such on shore: sound waves may be absorbed, masked, or distorted in the air due to surf and weather conditions. As he did in theaters and other auditoriums, Burris-Meyer provided a solution by synthesizing distinctive components of certain sounds, such as anchor chains dropping into the water, landing-craft engines, and tanks clanking up onto the beach, so that anybody along the shore would think they heard an approaching invasion. In April 1943 Bell Telephone Laboratories delivered the first field-ready Heater sonic projector. Contained in waterproof cases, it had a magnetic wire recorder, five-phase amplifier, 1,000-watt 12-horn speaker, and a 3hp Ohnen generator. The speakers were placed at the stern of the ARBs on swivel mounts to enable them to be always pointed toward the beach. Without the wind blowing it was found that the Heater was most effective when it was 660 yards offshore.

OPERATIONS

Sicily

In June 1943 BJU-1, ARB Squadron 1, and a few PT boats from RON-15 were designated Demonstration Group 80.4 at Bizerta, Tunisia, and sent to an advance base on the island of Pantelleria. Their task was to help keep a sizable portion of the German garrison in western Sicily as the Allies landed along the southern coast. Their planned first mission on July 10 off Cape San Marco, 100 miles west of the beachhead, was canceled due to rough seas and high winds. On the following night four ARBs successfully employed their Heaters, smoke pots, and rockets, and one PT boat fired its guns and rockets 3,000m off the beach while evading searchlights, machine-gun and artillery fire. On the night of July 12, DG 80.4 performed dual operations off Cape Granitola and Mazara del Vallo; the Germans announced the following day that an attempted landing in the area had been repelled. These deception operations were judged successful after one German division in reserve was held back from intervening against the actual Allied beachhead. As harbors on the island were liberated the Beach Jumpers contacted local fishermen to find out the location of offshore minefields. Their ARBs then cruised through them at 30 knots, causing the acoustic mines to detonate harmlessly 200–300ft behind them.

Although seen here on landing craft, these 1,000-watt 12-horn loudspeakers were normally mounted on "turnstiles" aboard Air-Sea Rescue Boats to project sonic deception toward shore in any direction. Beach Jumpers also read prepared scripts over the speakers, to simulate naval officers shouting orders to landing craft assembling offshore. (Author's photograph)

Italy

As part of the Allied invasion of Italy in September 1943, the renamed Diversion Task Group 80.4 was tasked to conduct diversionary operations north of Naples, and to seize several small islands in the Pontines group and in the Gulf of Naples. The destroyer USS *Knight*, two Dutch gunboats, several Royal Navy MLs, MTBs and sub-chasers were assigned to TG 80.4 for the operation. Just before midnight on September 8, TG 80.4 approached Ventotene shortly after the announcement of the Italian armistice. Accompanying them was author John Steinbeck, who was serving as a war correspondent for the *New York Herald Tribune*. Steinbeck had been asked to write a surrender demand that was broadcast over one of the ARB's speakers, warning the island's garrison that they would be bombarded if they did not capitulate in 15 minutes. Shortly afterward three white flares were fired from the island to signal its capitulation. TG 80.4 commander Capt Charles Andrews, accompanied by Lt Fairbanks, a small detachment from the Scout Co of 2nd Bn/509th Parachute Infantry, and a group of OSS agents, then landed on Ventotene. Italian forces on the island gave up immediately, while the Luftwaffe garrison in the hills surrendered the next day after being convinced that they were facing a far larger Allied force. The radar on the island was captured intact for examination by Allied technicians.

Meanwhile, several ARBs and a PT boat conducted a deception operation just south of the mouth of the Volturno river in the early hours of September 9, just as the US Fifth Army came ashore at Salerno. Two nights later TG 80.4 operated off Gaeta, 50 miles northwest of the beachhead, where an acoustic mine damaged an ARB, forcing them to shift their focus northwest to Cape Circio. The Germans reacted with a barrage of flares as intercepted radio transmissions revealed their frantic attempts to locate the landing craft that they believed were approaching. These efforts caused a Fallschirmjäger division to hesitate for several days before assisting in the defense of Salerno. On September 12, TG 80.4 occupied without opposition the island of Capri, and from there assisted with the uncontested seizure of neighboring islands, along with those in the nearby Pontines group. Admiral Hewitt disbanded TG 80.4 on September 18, and BJU-1 left Capri in November 1943 to return to Camp Bradford.

Southern France

On the night of June 16, 1944, BJU-5 aboard eight PT boats from RON-29 sailed from their base at Bastia on Corsica to conduct a deception operation off the northern coast of the island of Elba. With naval balloons floating behind them, in the early hours of June 17 the PT boats dropped a group of French Commandos of the Bataillon de Choc in rubber boats off Cape Enfola. BJU-5 then sailed east to Cape Vita to impersonate a large invasion force, using the "inflatable soldiers" for the first time. After receiving sporadic German shellfire, BJU-5 withdrew before dawn as the French Army landed successfully on the southern coast to liberate the island.

As part of Special Operations Task Group 80.4, the Beach Jumpers supported the landings between Toulon and Cannes in southern France in August 1944. The task group was divided for this operation. Western Diversionary Task Unit 80.4.1, under the command of task group commander Capt Henry C. Johnson, covered the left flank of the invasion area; it was composed of BJU-3, BJU-5, 12x ARBs, 8x PT boats, 4x Royal Navy MLs, and the destroyer USS *Endicott*. Eastern Diversionary Task Unit 80.4.2, under LtCdr Fairbanks, was responsible for the right flank, and had BJU-1, 22x PT boats, 4x Royal Navy MLs, and the gunboats HMS *Aphis* and HMS *Scarab*. Some German radar sites in southern France were left untargeted by the preliminary bombardment to enable them to detect and report on the deception operations.

In the early hours of August 15, TG 80.4.1 sailed between Marseilles and Toulon, with the USS *Endicott* shelling Ciotat Bay and sinking a German merchantman. Visibility and navigation problems caused by heavy fog forced some ARBs to operate further down the coast from where they had planned; these actions suitably alerted the Germans, who responded with their shore batteries. Meanwhile, four PT boats from TG 80.4.2 put French Commandos ashore at Pointe des Deux Frères near Cannes, while HMS *Aphis* and HMS *Scarab* bombarded targets between Nice and Cannes. With the main landings under way, TG 80.4.1 and TG 80.4.2 rendezvoused to again conduct a diversionary operation off Ciotat Bay in the early morning of August 16. As gunboats bombarded targets, three waves of ARBs raced into the bay under the cover of their smokescreens, operating their Heaters and unleashing rockets; the Germans replied with star shells, searchlights, and artillery fire. To cover their withdrawal the last few boats dropped smoke pots and delayed-action explosive charges that went off at intervals for 15 minutes. As a result, German forces around Ciotat Bay were not only kept in place but were reinforced with units that would otherwise have contested the actual Allied landings.

Just before dawn on August 16 several ARBs encountered two Kriegsmarine corvettes, the ex-Egyptian *Kemid Allah* (U-Jäger 6083) and the ex-Italian *Capaiuolo* (U-Jäger 6071) that were each armed with three radar-controlled 4.7in guns. Rapidly zigzagging and laying smoke, the outgunned ARBs radioed for help; in response, Fairbanks aboard HMS *Aphis* led HMS *Scarab* into a ferocious gun battle that saw their radio

HMS *Aphis* was a World War I-vintage Royal Navy gunboat that served as LtCdr Fairbanks' flagship when he commanded Eastern Diversionary Task Unit 80.4.2 during Operation "Dragoon." After conducting diversionary bombardments along the French coast it helped sink two German corvettes after a furious naval duel. (Imperial War Museum A 17372, via Douglas Fairbanks Jr Collection, Howard Gotlieb Archival Research Center, Boston University)

antennas and gun sights shot away. With the ARBs safely away the gunboats began ducking in and out of the smoke, waiting for their overheating 3in guns to cool enough to continue firing. The destroyer USS *Endicott* soon arrived and sank both corvettes with only three of its crewmen slightly wounded, while the Beach Jumpers suffered no casualties. For its role in the success of Operation "Dragoon," TG 80.4.1 received the Presidential Unit Citation; Fairbanks himself received the Legion of Merit for the deception operations he had planned, and for his role in the sinking of the corvettes.

The Philippines

The Beach Jumpers did not operate in the Pacific until the liberation of Luzon in the Philippines in January 1945. In November 1944, BJU-6 and BJU-7 became a part of Diversionary Task Group 77.11 at Milne Bay in New Guinea; this command included LCI Flotilla 24 and PT boat squadrons RON-8, RON-24, and RON-25. On December 30 a kamikaze hit the PT tender USS *Orestes*, killing and wounding several leading officers from TG 77.11 just after the ship arrived at their new base at Mangarin Bay on Mindoro; this attack prevented TG 77.11 from participating in the landings at Lingayen Gulf on January 9, 1945.

Later that month the task group was directed to feign an amphibious landing off Tayabas Bay in southern Luzon; this was intended to distract the Japanese from the forthcoming landings at Zambales on January 29 to cut off the Bataan Peninsula, and at Nasugbu Bay south of Manila on January 31. On the night of January 22/23, TG 77.11 divided into two task units that sailed in opposite directions along the bay between Calotan and Mabio Point. Beach Jumpers operating from the LCI(L)s jammed Japanese radar while broadcasting fake radio traffic to simulate a landing force. Along with the LCI(L)s the supporting PT boats had corner reflectors, smoke generators, and smoke pots to shield their true identity while rockets were fired at the shore. Just after midnight the LCI(L)s began releasing meteorological balloons with attached corner reflectors at two-minute intervals, until each craft had released five balloons. Both task units then returned separately to Mangarin Bay. TG 77.11 returned to Tayabas Bay on the night of January 30/31, this time dividing into three task units to repeat the same operation. As a result of what would become the last Beach Jumper operation of the war, at least two Japanese divisions were prevented from moving against the actual landings to the north of them.

NAVAL COMBAT DEMOLITION UNITS

Forerunners: North Africa & Sicily

Successful amphibious assaults needed to overcome any natural and man-made obstacles that would hinder their ability to reach and move inland from the beach. As the Allies prepared to invade French North Africa, an important airfield near Port Lyautey in Morocco had to be seized; the only approach to it was up the Sebou river, which was blocked by a cable boom near its mouth. The US Navy hastily formed and trained its first demolition unit to blast through the barrier so the destroyer USS *Dallas* could pass through and land its US Army detachment to occupy the airfield.

ABOVE
Seen here at Fort Pierce, FL, LtCdr Draper Kauffman is considered the father of naval combat demolition; his tough training regimen and spirit of teamwork molded volunteers into effective demolition units. Despite graduating from the Naval Academy in 1933 he was kept out of the service until shortly before Pearl Harbor due to his poor eyesight. During the war Kauffman was rarely photographed wearing his glasses, even though he had to tape them directly to his head while swimming off Saipan and Tinian. Kauffman later commanded UDTs off Iwo Jima and Okinawa. (National UDT-SEAL Museum)

RIGHT
Although NCDUs, such as these sailors posing at Fort Pierce, were equipped with and instructed in the use of small arms, the highly trained demolitioneers were strongly encouraged to focus on their primary specialty and to avoid direct combat whenever possible. (National UDT-SEAL Museum)

The all-volunteer Naval Demolition Unit coordinated its first attempt with a small group of US Army engineers on the first night of the invasion, November 8, 1942. Approaching the boom aboard an LCVP from the attack transport USS *George Clymer*, they were turned back by heavy French machine-gun fire from the shore. On the following night the NDU arrived at the boom alone and undetected after failing to rendezvous with US Army engineers. They breached the boom with explosives, but this part of the river seemed too shallow for the USS *Dallas* to negotiate, and machine-gun fire from the nearby Kasbah fort forced the NDU to withdraw with several wounded. The remnants of the boom, stretching halfway across the river from its southern bank, were easily overcome a few hours later by the USS *Dallas* steaming at full speed, resulting in the quick capture of the airfield, and every member of the NDU received the Navy Cross.

One more temporary demolition unit, made up of Seabees (men from Naval Construction Battalions) with explosives training, was quickly formed and trained in clearing beach obstacles in May 1943 in preparation for the invasion of Sicily, under the designation Naval Demolition Unit 1. In the event it was not needed to perform its intended function that July, when US troops failed to encounter any beach obstacles as they waded ashore, but NDU 1 did demolish piles of rubble and barricades that blocked several exits off the beach.

Establishment of NCDUs
The permanent establishment of naval demolition units was authorized in May 1943 to deal with the expected multitude of beach obstacles along the Normandy coast. Lieutenant Draper Kauffman's experience in defusing unexploded bombs in London (while serving in the Royal Navy) and at Pearl Harbor, plus his founding of the US Naval Bomb Disposal School, led to him being assigned to set up a combat demolitions school at Fort Pierce,

Florida that June. When they were officially organized the following September as NCDUs, their size was determined by the capacity of the LCR(S) they operated from. Each was originally composed of one officer, six enlisted men and their explosives, but one man was subsequently cut from each NCDU so the LCR(S) could carry more demolition materials.

Weapons & equipment

NCDUs used standard-issue explosives such as TNT, tetrytol, C-2 plastic composition, and primacord (instantaneous detonating cord) to demolish natural and man-made beach obstacles. They also improvised their own explosive devices, such as the Mk 8 demolition hose; numbers of this 2in-diameter floatable rubber tube, 25ft long and filled with 50lb of tetrytol, were often used after amphibious landings in the Pacific to clear obstacles and blow channels through sandbars and coral reefs. Paths through such obstacles were also blasted with crates of Bangalore torpedoes fused together as massive explosive blocks. Mark 8 demolition hoses were also employed to clear wrecked landing craft left on Omaha Beach in Normandy.

In the spring of 1944 an NCDU officer in Britain, Lt Carl P. Hagensen, invented a demolition charge that could overcome the large German "Belgian Gate" beach obstacles without spreading deadly shrapnel around. Called the Hagensen Pack, each contained 2¼lb of C-2 sewn into a foot-long canvas bag with a metal hook and a sash cord so that it could be attached to almost any part of an obstacle, and the flexibility of the C-2 also allowed it to be wrapped around a beam or pole. A length of primacord was placed

Some of the demolition materials used by both NCDUs and UDTs (see also Plate F2). Half-pound blocks of TNT are stacked on the box at upper left. On the right-hand box is a spool of instantaneous detonating cord (primacord), next to M1 demolition chains made up of TNT blocks in series sewn into cloth covers and linked by primacord, for packing in satchel charges. Among items recognizable in the foreground are (from left to right): a ½lb can of Dupont cap sealing compound; propped against the lying canister, four T-shaped friction-pull 30-second delay M1 fuse-lighters; a stack of Herco-Tube containers for electric blasting caps (detonators); a drilled-block wooden box and a cardboard pack with Atlas brand non-electric "special" blasting caps; and in the center foreground, a 100ft coil of Clover brand safety fuse in a clear plastic cover. (NARA)

In September 1944, members of an NCDU prepare Mk 8 demolition hoses aboard an LCI(D) for a demolition operation off Morotai island. These 25ft-long rubber tubes were each filled with 50lb of tetrytol explosive. (NARA)

As they are being prepared to blow a channel through a reef off Morotai island, these Mk 8 rubber demolition hoses are being tied together with primacord (which was waterproof): square knots were used, since granny knots posed a greater risk of a misfire. It was always normal practice to duplicate primacord links and blasting caps where possible. (NARA)

inside the C-2, with the remaining length wrapped around the bag so that it could be connected quickly to the main "trunk line" linking several targets for simultaneous destruction. Due to the size of the charge a Hagensen Pack was only effective when it was placed near a mine or over a joint or weld of an obstacle. It was soon determined that 16 strategically placed packs could safely destroy a "Belgian Gate," and to ensure that enough were ready for D-Day makeshift packs were made up with C-2 and a foot of primacord placed in GI-issue wool socks that could be attached to obstacles with friction tape, twine, or wire. Friction-pull M1 delayed fuse lighters (wrapped in condoms for waterproofing) were used to detonate the Hagensen Pack, the success of which on D-Day led the US Navy to officially adopt it as the Mk 20 Demolition Charge.

OPERATIONS:

PACIFIC

In January 1944 the first of ten NCDUs began arriving at Turner City on Florida Island in the Solomons. NCDU-4 and NCDU-5 were the first to see action, on February 15, when they supported the 3rd New Zealand Division's landing on Green Island north of Bougainville. They succeeded in blasting coral-heads in the harbor, but strong currents thwarted their attempts to blast a channel to its entrance. In late March the two NCDUs made a reconnaissance of the abandoned Emirau Island, and cleared its harbor as the Marines occupied it. In June, NCDUs 12, 13, 14, and 15 were temporarily assigned to Underwater Demolition Teams 3, 4, 5, and 7 respectively for the Marianas campaign (see below). The following month all ten NCDUs at Turner City were consolidated into Team Able in preparation for the landings on Peleliu. Unfortunately Team Able lost all of its equipment after their transport ship, the USS *Noa*, collided with the destroyer USS *Fullam* before the start of the operation. All the NCDU personnel survived, and were subsequently sent to Maui to be integrated into the UDTs.

Five NCDUs were assigned to the Seventh Amphibious Force, and operated in LCMs from LCI(D)s that each carried two NCDUs and 40 tons of explosives. They scouted beaches, blew up natural and man-made obstacles, blasted channels to the beachheads, and cleared harbors of obstructions. On March 6, 1944, NCDU-2 blew a channel through a reef along the northern coast of Los Negros in the Admiralty Islands to allow reinforcements from the 1st Cavalry Division to relieve its "reconnaissance in force," whose defensive perimeter was being hard pressed on the eastern coast. All five NCDUs assisted Gen MacArthur's leapfrogging campaign

LCI(D) 227 was a converted landing craft that transported NCDU-19 and NCDU-21, along with 40 tons of explosives, along the northern coast of New Guinea and to Leyte in the Philippines during the summer and fall of 1944. (National UDT-SEAL Museum)

Two men from NCDU-19 somewhere in the southwest Pacific. They are wearing the Jack Browne rig (left) and the Munson Lung (right); these were used by swimmers when placing explosives on submerged reefs, sandbars, and sunken vessels to clear channels to the beach. Note that the Jack Browne rig is a self-contained rebreather system, while the Munson Lung required air lines to an electrically powered air-compressor on the surface. (National UDT-SEAL Museum)

along the northern coast of New Guinea that year, supporting the landings at Hollandia, Aitape, Biak, Noemfoor, and Morotai. On October 18/19 the NCDUs assisted the UDTs in surveying the beaches at San Pedro Bay near Tacloban on Leyte in the Philippines. The NCDUs continued to support the campaign to liberate the rest of the archipelago, with the Omaha Beach veterans NCDU-24 joining them for the landing on Palawan on February 28, 1945. In late April four NCDUs assisted the Royal Australian Engineers in surveying the beaches at Tarakan in Borneo, and demolishing several rows of wooden stakes along with wire and iron obstacles behind a smokescreen when Australian infantry landed there on May 1. Their final operation occurred when NCDU-2 and NCDU-3, operating alongside UDT-11, supported the Australian landings at Brunei Bay in June 1945.

D. NAVAL COMBAT DEMOLITION UNITS, 1944

1: Demolitioneer, NCDU-19; Morotai island, September 1944
As the Allies leapfrogged along the top of New Guinea, NCDUs demolished any natural obstacles encountered after the initial landings to clear the way for incoming supplies and reinforcements. The NCDU personnel had to be constantly on the alert not only for stay-behind Japanese snipers in trees above the beaches, but also for sharks in the shallows; they were ready to throw grenades, or anything else that came to hand, to keep them at a distance. Wearing just an HBT field cap and trousers cut down into shorts, this demolitioneer is laying three Mk 8 demolition hoses along a sandbar.

2: "Gap team" member, Special Engineer Task Force; Omaha Beach, Normandy, June 6, 1944
The Gap teams of the SETF that assaulted Omaha Beach were composed of both NCDUs and US Army engineers. This Navy member of one team can be identified by the gray stripe painted round the base of his M1 helmet to distinguish him from the soldiers on the beach. He is hurriedly running a ring of primacord around a group of obstacles; this will be connected by other lengths of primacord to the explosives placed on the obstacles by his teammates, so that they can be demolished simultaneously.

3: NCDU, Beach Obstacle Demolition Party; Utah Beach, June 6, 1944
The BODPs that landed on Utah Beach were able to methodically clear all the obstacles off the beach with less difficulty and loss, thanks to the accurate preliminary bombardment that subdued the German defenses. This NCDU of a BODP is about to detonate a group of obstacles by twisting the handle of his blasting machine; two-strand telephone wire connects the "hell box" to an electric blasting cap that is taped to the "ring main" of primacord linking the charges fitted to the obstacles. The US Army M2 ammo vest that he is wearing contains Hagensen Packs that will be placed on other obstacles; **3a** shows one of them, here the makeshift version produced in quantity for D-Day from GI wool socks filled with C-2 plastic explosive.

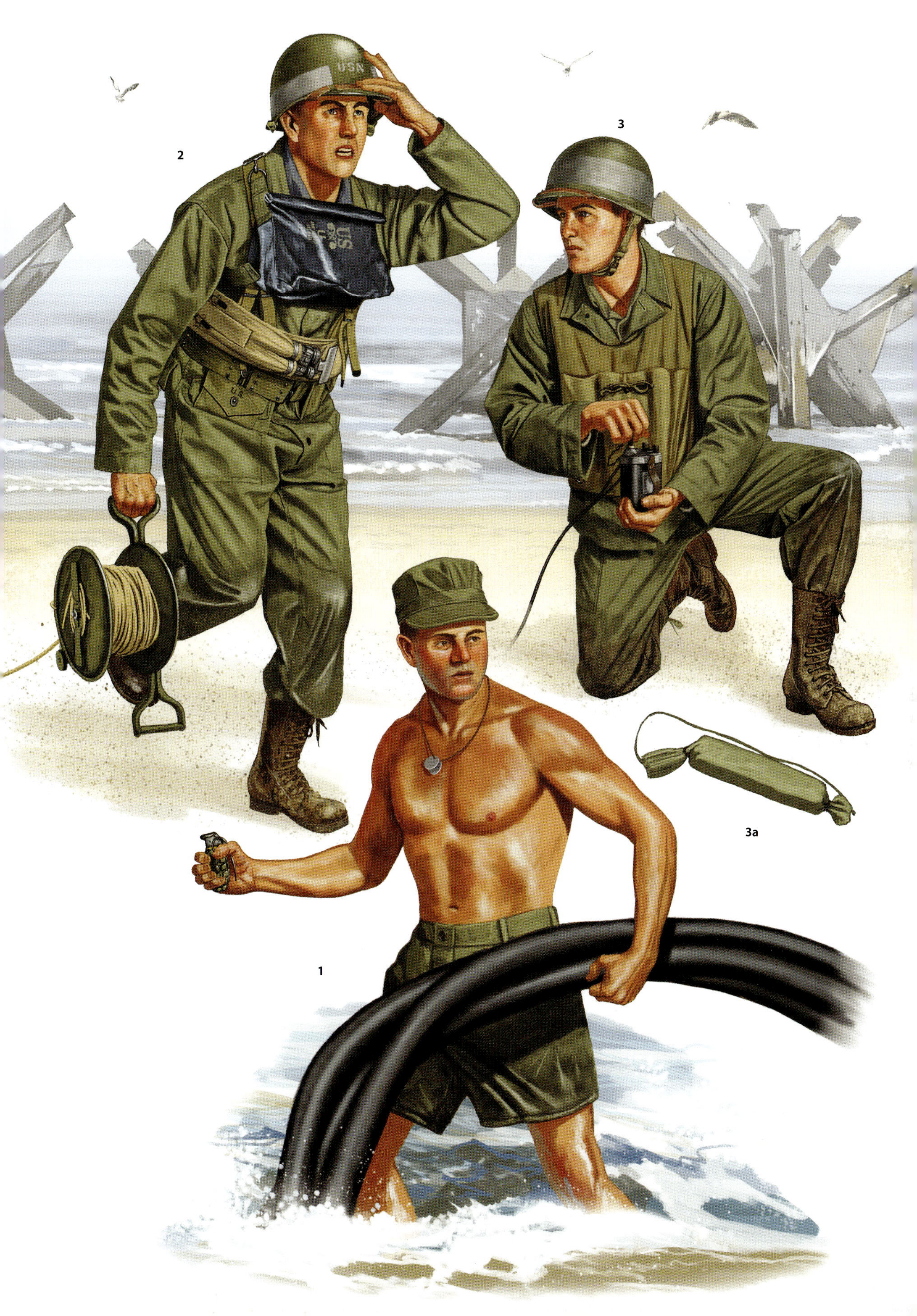

2
3
3a
1
USN
US

Normandy: tetrahedrons and "Belgian Gates" in the foreground, along with "Czech Hedgehogs" in the background, cover a typical stretch of beach backed by bluffs somewhere along the coastline. This array was similar to that which greeted many US Gap and BODP teams as they stepped off their landing craft on D-Day. (National UDT-SEAL Museum)

EUROPE

By March 1944 the Germans commanded by Field Marshal Erwin Rommel had placed enough beach obstacles in Normandy to make the Allies alter their plans for the cross-Channel invasion. The US Army had originally wanted a night landing at high tide so that there would be less distance for the assault infantry to cross to reach the top of the beach, and that under the cover of darkness. The obstacles, however, forced the Allies to land at low tide, just as the early-morning daylight revealed them, so that the NCDUs would have time to blow gaps through them to allow following landing craft to reach shore. Taking into account the parallel requirement for a full moon to illuminate the airborne landings, the date for Operation "Overlord" was tentatively set for early June.

In this drawing entitled "Naval Demolition Units Reaching Beach," by Lt Mitchell Jaimeson, a Gap team drag their explosives-laden rubber boats onto Omaha Beach on D-Day. These boats were quickly abandoned when they attracted heavy German fire. (National UDT-SEAL Museum)

Despite the hurried deployment of NCDUs to Britain, the density of obstacles on Omaha and Utah beaches, along with the limited amount of time that would be available for demolition as the tide rose, prompted a decision to form joint US Army/Navy Gap teams. Each team comprised a 26-man US Army engineer unit, and a 13-man NCDU composed of the original six demolitioneers augmented with US Navy recruits to handle the rubber LCR(S)s. The US Army's 146th and 299th Engineer Bns supplied men for the 21 Gap teams that landed on Omaha Beach as part of V Corps' Special Engineer Task Force. For the VII Corps assault on Utah Beach, men from the 237th and 299th Engineer Bns expanded the NCDUs into 12 Beach Obstacle Demolition Parties (BODPs). These demolition units were to land after the first wave of infantry to blow gaps in the obstacles for the following waves.

Omaha Beach

Omaha Beach was about 7,000 yards long, 400 yards wide at low tide, and 200 yards wide at high tide. It had two rows of obstacles that were each 50–75 yards wide. The first row, 250 yards below the high-water line, was composed of metal "Belgian Gates" along with wooden ramps and stakes with Teller mines mounted on top. The second row also had wooden stakes and ramps, along with three rows of tripod-like metal "Czech Hedgehogs." Through these the Gap teams were to blow 16 breaches, each 50 yards wide and 350 yards long – while the Germans fired down upon them from the bluffs and cliffs above. The NCDUs were to start at the water's edge and work their way up the beach, while the US Army engineers were to begin at the obstacles halfway toward the seawall. With the first wave set to land at 0630hrs and the tide rising a foot every eight minutes, the Gap teams had only 30 minutes to demolish the first row of obstacles before it was covered by water.

In his drawing "Naval Demolition Men Blowing Up Obstacles," Jaimeson depicts a Gap team placing explosives on a "Czech Hedgehog" surrounded by the carnage on Omaha Beach. Various other types of beach obstacles are visible in this scene. (National UDT-SEAL Museum)

Despite their imposing size, "Belgian Gates" had the unpleasant property of allowing small-arms fire to pass directly through them, to the peril of Gap teams working on them. Mitchell Jaimeson's drawing "Placing a Charge on a Belgian Gate" illustrates the risk these men faced as they necessarily worked bunched closely together. (Navy Art Collection, Naval History and Heritage Command)

The teams crossed the English Channel the night before D-Day in LCT(A)s that each towed an LCM containing a rubber LCR(S) loaded with 500lb of explosives, primacord, and Bangalore torpedoes; these rubber boats were to be dragged onto the beach. As the LCMs approached Omaha Beach, their navigation was hindered by the coastal cross-currents and the smoke caused by the naval bombardment. Most of the Gap teams landed on the eastern half of Omaha Beach, 10–15 minutes behind schedule. Machine-gun fire and shrapnel immediately brought down many demolitioneers and engineers as they left their LCMs; others abandoned their LCR(S)s when mortar fire started to hit the explosives in them, killing and wounding everyone nearby. The depleted teams, wet and seasick, found themselves mixed up with one another, and pooled their scattered explosives together to fulfill their mission as best they could. Mortar fire prematurely set off explosives placed on the obstacles, wiping out groups of demolitioneers while they worked. The blowing of the charges was hampered by rising water, by soldiers taking cover behind the obstacles, and by primacord lines being severed by German fire, landing craft, or the few tanks and other vehicles that made it onto the beach. Short on time and patience, some demolitioneers set their fuses to motivate soldiers to move away from the obstacles, and infantrymen quickly learned to avoid Gap teams entirely, since they attracted the heaviest fire. A few cleared gaps were later blocked by sunken landing craft, while obstacles hidden by the rising tide sank or severely damaged incoming assault landing craft and prevented others from landing reinforcements.

Amid all this chaos, half of the Gap teams were able to blow five channels through the obstacles, mostly in the Easy Red sector between the St Laurent and Colleville exits, but just two gaps were made on the western side of Omaha Beach. When the German defenders were finally overcome, and after the tide receded again, more gaps were made that afternoon with bulldozers and salvaged explosives. The obstacles, along with the wreckage, soon disappeared as the demolitioneers worked to improve the flow of men and material moving inland.

Although they did not prevent American troops from reaching the beach, the obstacles did succeed in forcing the first wave to land several hundred yards further away from the high-water line and to endure a much longer ordeal under German firepower. Given the limited time the tide allowed, and the heavy enemy fire, the expectation that the Gap teams would be able to clear all 16 channels on the morning of D-Day was overly optimistic, and the price they paid for what they did achieve was heavy. Of the 190 NCDU demolitioneers in the Gap teams on Omaha Beach, 32 were killed and 65 were wounded; seven received the Navy Cross, while the entire NCDU contingent received the Presidential Unit Citation.

The watercolor "Demolition Crew at Work, Frejus Beach, France" by Albert K. Murray depicts NCDUs placing explosives on submerged obstacles in the Golfe de Frejus after the landings in southern France. (Navy Art Collection, Naval History and Heritage Command)

Utah Beach

In contrast to Omaha Beach, the BODP teams faced the less daunting though still dangerous mission of clearing the scant number of obstacles spread out sporadically along the 700-yard stretch of Utah Beach. Although the obstacles did not pose a significant impediment to the landing forces (none of them had Teller mines attached to them), 12 BODP teams demolished them so they would not be a hindrance to the following waves. Crossing the channel in LSTs, the BODPs pulled their LCR(S)s full of explosives onto the beach from LCVPs just after the first wave landed at around 0600 hours. By 0800hrs the modest number of obstacles had been cleared up to the barbed wire in front of the seawall, which was subsequently breached by Army engineers. The task was made easier by the relative accuracy of the massive naval and aerial bombardment on Utah Beach, which reduced the level of German resistance to sporadic machine-gun, rocket, and long-range artillery fire; two NCDU men were killed and 14 wounded. For their efforts the NCDUs on Utah Beach received the only Navy Unit Commendation awarded for D-Day. In the following days the demolitioneers helped clear the beach of obstructions while others followed the assault wave inland to neutralize bunkers and pillboxes, including one that was still calling down artillery fire on the beachhead on D+1. Many of the NCDUs then departed for Salerno, in preparation for the invasion of southern France in August.

Southern France: radio-controlled "drones"

Since the Mediterranean coastline did not experience any tidal fluctuations, all the mined rows of wooden posts and concrete tetrahedrons in front of the designated landing areas between Toulon and Cannes remained submerged just below the surface. About 30 NCDU teams were assigned to support the American forces landing on August 15, 1944 in the Alpha, Delta, and Camel sectors. They were to blow gaps through the obstacles with radio-controlled Apex boats; launched from an LST, the Apex might be compared to what we call today a "drone": it was an LCVP filled with high explosives, which was controlled remotely with radio signals from a command boat. The "male" version of the Apex was loaded with one ton of explosives, to create an initial breach in the obstacles just big enough for the following "female" Apex to penetrate to blow a bigger gap with its four-ton load.

At 0715hrs in the Alpha sector, the Apex boats exploded amongst the obstacles along the left side of Red Beach in the Baie de Cavalaire. Although some gaps and mines were blown, the right side of Red Beach was untouched, and was therefore closed after mines damaged several landing craft when they reached it at 0800 hours. At the same time, along Yellow Beach in the Baie de Pampelonne, Apex boats exploded against the obstacles despite one running aground, one sinking, and one turning back out to sea before exploding and disabling a submarine-chaser. The gaps made were just sufficient for the landing craft to reach the beaches, and the NCDUs paddled in rubber boats to the remaining rows of obstacles to clear them away with hand-placed charges. The lack of obstacles in front of the landing beaches east of Sainte-Maxime, in the Delta sector along the Baie de Bougnon, forestalled the need for Apexes to be used there ahead of the landings.

In the Camel sector, the defenses were strongest around Red Beach west of Saint Raphaël, with a large offshore minefield, numerous coastal batteries, and two rows of mined concrete tetrahedrons. At 1300hrs Apexes were sent against the offshore obstacles, but were forced back by brackets of near-misses from German batteries. On the second attempt they pressed on under fire, but then began moving about in irregular patterns as they failed to obey radio commands. Two were re-boarded by the NCDUs, two ran aground on the beach, one ran wild and was sunk by the destroyer USS *Ordronaux*, while three did explode amongst the obstacles. Their inability to clear the obstacles, along with the failure of the sea and air bombardment to neutralize the enemy artillery, led to the 142nd Infantry Regiment being landed instead at the already secured Green Beach east of Saint Raphael at 1530 hours.

It was suspected that the radio frequencies used to control the Apex boats were susceptible to jamming by the Germans and to interference from frequencies used by the invasion fleet. For the next several days NCDUs cleared the remaining offshore obstacles and mines along with the beached Apex craft. NCDUs also removed obstructions from the harbors, including St Tropez, to allow the landings of the French II Corps.

UNDERWATER DEMOLITION TEAMS

When the Pacific Fleet began its advance across the central Pacific, intelligence on coral reefs, tides, and Japanese defenses on atolls to be seized was obtained from pre-war inhabitants and photographs taken by reconnaissance planes and submarines. However, these sources could only offer estimates on the extent and nature of the natural barriers the invasion forces would face between the line of departure and the beach. Plans for a special group of scout swimmers were just being put forward when these shortcomings proved tragically evident, when the Marines landed on Tarawa on November 20, 1943. The planners had overestimated the water depth in the lagoon where the landings took place, and while the first wave of LVT "amtracs" made it to shore, the low tide caused the following LCVPs to run aground at the edge of the surrounding coral reef. Forced to wade ashore over long distances under heavy fire, many Marines were cut down before they reached the beach. The massive casualties sustained in taking Tarawa expedited plans for the formation of UDT-1 and UDT-2 at the Waimanalo Amphibious Training Base on Oahu in Hawaii that December, from volunteers with experience in explosives from all the armed services.

Weapons & equipment

One weapon each UDT swimmer always carried was a knife that primarily served as a multipurpose cutting tool. The first one issued was the 10.13in-long US Navy Mk 1 KA-BAR knife with a 5.25in blade and a hilt made from either aluminum, plastic, steel, or wood. The 12in-long Mk 2 KA-BAR with a 7in blade was also issued, but its carbon steel blade rusted from the constant exposure to saltwater. Union Cutlery made an improved version with all metal components in bright chrome to keep corrosion to a minimum; called the Bright Mk 2, this knife also had a varnished leather hilt for added protection from saltwater.

The UDTs first used goggles at Kwajalein, but these were soon discarded after they proved difficult to keep completely clear and presented a distorted underwater view. The dive mask offered a clear view, but there was some hesitation in adopting it due to a fear that the reflection from its large single

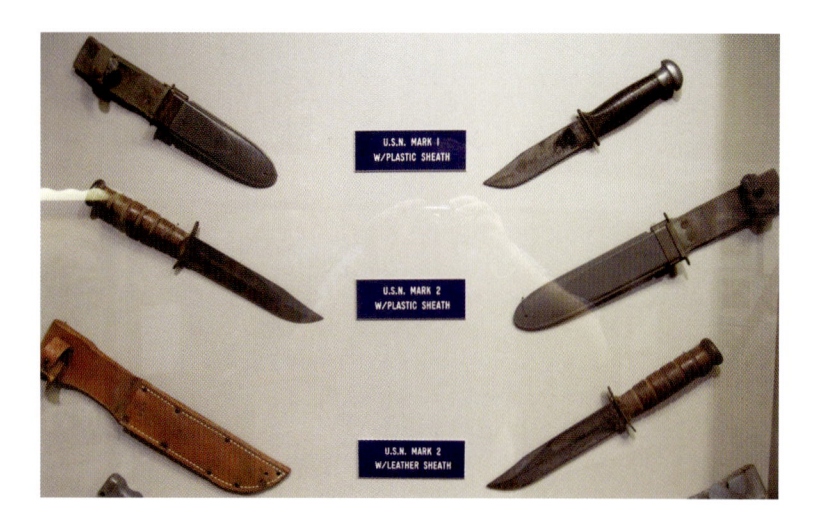

UDT swimmers carried their Mk 1 (top) and Mk 2 knives (center & bottom) in gray plastic scabbards during operations after soaking in seawater caused the standard-issue leather sheaths to fall apart. (Author's photograph)

glass plate would attract enemy fire. The UDTs soon bought up all the dive masks they could locate from sporting goods companies. Since they were made in one particular size in hard rubber, sandpaper was used to make the masks fit more comfortably to individual faces. To prevent the mask from leaking its loose glass plate was sealed.

Swim fins were initially rejected because the early models were made of a hard rubber that chafed the ankles, made walking in them difficult, and made carving the owner's initials in them a strenuous chore. Swimming with the hard rubber fins with stiff legs led to painful cramps. When personnel from the OSS MU joined the UDTs in mid-1944, they demonstrated how to swim sidestroke with a more flexible Owen Churchill model of swim fins that prevented cramps and did not churn up telltale wakes. Swim fins thus became standard issue by late 1944, and some were lengthened with vulcanized rubber extensions.

To survey water depth along the approaches that landing craft would take toward the beach, UDTs used a reel with about 1,000ft of fishing-line knotted every 25 feet. Starting at a buoy placed at the end of the reef, a pair of swimmers would unroll the line from a reel made out of two 4in milk cans welded together with a round wooden flange at each end. At each knot, one swimmer would drop a 10ft-long length of fishing-line marked off at 1ft intervals and with a lead sinker at its end. This was done to measure the

Aboard an APD fast transport, a swimmer from a UDT uses black electrical tape to attach a length of primacord to a tetrytol block. Eight of these blocks would fit into one of the satchel charges that are being stockpiled behind him. (NARA)

water depth, which was then recorded on a Plexiglas slate with a grease pencil. The other swimmer would also take note of any natural or man-made obstructions at the same spot. Their APD transport would meanwhile be taking radar bearings on each of the buoys, so all the surveys between them and the beach could be accurately charted.

The M1 chain demolition satchel charge was the primary tool used to clear beaches of obstacles. Each was a canvas haversack containing eight 11in blocks of tetrytol linked together through their centers on a 16ft length of primacord (the heat in the Pacific theater made composition C plastic explosive potentially too dangerous to use). The alternative Mk 133 demolition charge had eight 12in blocks of TNT cast around a 25ft length of primacord. A flotation bladder was included in its canvas haversack so that swimmers could tow a row of them toward shore, then puncture the bladders to sink them as needed. The charges would be attached to an obstacle with wire, friction tape, or large rubber bands cut from old inner tubes, and were so placed that the debris from the demolition would fall in the direction of the beach. The 2½ft length of primacord protruding from the end of the chain of charges would then be tied to the master "trunk line" or "ring main," which was composed of two strands of primacord strung along the tops of the separate obstacles from opposite ends of the area of operation. Late in the war, UDTs carried 20 Hagensen Packs in the Mk 127 demolition charge; based on the US Army's M2 ammunition vest, this had a large pocket on its front and back (see Plate D3).

When a Japanese anti-boat mine was encountered, a ½lb block of tetrytol with a long fuse was tied to one of its horns to detonate it, but this proved to be ineffective if the mine itself was not already armed. UDTs were then issued the Mk 1 "destructor" composed of a blasting cap, a spring clip, and a time pencil; this would be attached directly to the mine's horn to detonate the mine after the appropriate delay. A swimmer would carry ten of these destructors in the belt-shaped Mk 136 demolition outfit.

At low tide on Peleliu, a swimmer from UDT-7 is about to place a charge on a Japanese J-13 anti-boat mine. The length of primacord already strung across it will serve as the "trunk line," to detonate this mine simultaneously with all the other obstructions on the beach. (National UDT-SEAL Museum)

Once the explosives were placed on the obstacles and connected to the main trunk line, another line of primacord connected to it was attached to a fuse igniter on a wooden board floating just offshore (this arrangement was often duplicated in case one failed). The time-delay igniter was either the Mk 12 or Mk 15 firing device, with a spring-activated firing pin; the Mk 12 could be set for delays of between 5 and 92 seconds, the Mk 15 between 15 minutes and 11 hours. Although both were effective to about 25ft underwater, they were waterproofed with condoms to guarantee ignition. The swimmer who swam the fastest was made the "fuse puller"; he made sure the fuses were working properly once their safety pins were pulled, and was the last man recovered before the explosives went off simultaneously.

Transportation

Each UDT was composed of 13 officers and 85 men, divided into four platoons each with two officers and 15 men plus one headquarters platoon with five officers and 25 men. Initial operations in the Marshall Islands encountered serious delays when UDT personnel and their equipment were placed aboard several different transports. Thereafter, each UDT was transported across the Pacific in its own APD, a specially modified World War I-vintage destroyer. Its depth-charge racks, torpedo tubes, two forward stacks along with the corresponding boilers in the forward fireroom were all removed to accommodate the 95 bunks; these were stacked 5ft high, with the bottom 2ft of the compartment used for storing the tetrytol explosive. Life aboard the APDs was cramped until more spacious destroyer escorts were converted later in the war. Davits were added for the four LCP(R)s used by the UDT for its operations. Armed with 3x 3in guns, 2x 40mm guns, and 5x 20mm guns, the APD could provide covering fire to its swimmers. However, having APDs use their firepower to perform standard picket duty for the fleet in hostile waters when not engaged in UDT operations placed too many highly trained specialists in needless danger from air attack, as was tragically demonstrated late in the war.

Sailing toward the Marianas on the port beam of the battleship USS *California* in June 1944, the USS *Dickerson* was an elderly Wickes-class destroyer converted into an APD fast transport as used by the UDTs. The landing craft amidships supported UDT-3 during its operations off Guam the following month. The USS *Dickerson* was later crippled by two kamikazes off Okinawa in April 1945, and was subsequently towed out to sea and sunk. (NARA)

This LCP(R) is being lowered into the water before an operation off Saipan. Personnel from the UDT's headquarters platoon manned these landing craft, to guarantee better coordination between swimmers and support craft. Note the inflatable "surfboard" on the stern, a rubber flotation device shared with the UDTs by the OSS Maritime Unit. Inflatable in minutes with a compressed-air cylinder, the 10ft 6in-long, 3ft-wide surfboard weighed 310lb and, propelled by an electric motor at 5 knots, could carry two men and their equipment up to a total load of 900lb. Unfortunately, when they were used at Saipan they attracted heavy Japanese fire, and were discarded thereafter. (NARA)

From their APD, the UDT swimmers were carried to and from hostile shores in LCP(R)s. These were initially armed with two .30cal machine guns mounted in the bow tubs, until they were replaced with .50cal machine guns at bow and stern for greater range and rate of fire. (Late in the war these would be mounted on the APDs, to thicken up their anti-kamikaze defense between operations.)

Arriving at the designated position one at a time to avoid the appearance of an actual landing, each LCP(R) carried a platoon of 14 UDT swimmers, who entered the water over the seaward side via a rubber boat lashed alongside the landing craft. The LCP(R) followed a zigzag pattern at its top speed of 9 knots while dropping pairs of swimmers off at 100-yard intervals; it then cruised in figure-of-eight patterns just off the beach to provide covering fire. A "swimming officer" aboard the LCP(R), with binoculars and access to the boat's SCR-536 and SCR-610 radios, would report the progress of the operation back to the APD, and call in fire support from nearby ships if necessary. He also spotted swimmers waiting to be picked up, usually in a straight line at 25-yard intervals. Cruising at flank speed, LCP(R)s recovered

ABOVE
Most swimmers wore M1 helmets while aboard their landing craft as a precaution against incoming fire while cruising to and from enemy-defended beaches. Ironically, the UDTs suffered more casualties from Japanese air attacks on their APDs than during their scouting and demolition missions. (National UDT-SEAL Museum)

RIGHT
March 31, 1945: note that this LCP(R) has a rubber LCR(L) lashed to its side as it prepares to deploy its swimmers off Okinawa, while Japanese positions are bombarded in the background. Swimmers always entered the water from the side of the landing craft facing away from the enemy-held shore. (National UDT-SEAL Museum)

their swimmers by hand or with a double-looped rubber snare that quickly got them aboard the rubber boat. Many LCP(R)s performed fake cast-and-recovery missions off various beaches of a targeted island to confuse the Japanese, who were reluctant to open fire and reveal their positions prematurely.

OPERATIONS

The Marshalls

UDT-1 and UDT-2 were trained on Oahu to measure the water depth and look for obstacles by wading to the edge of the beach while wearing fatigues and tethered by a line to a rubber boat or an LCVP. Their first objective was Kwajalein Atoll in the Marshall Islands, with Kwajalein Island at its southeast corner and Roi-Namur on the northern edge.

On the morning of January 31, 1944, UDT-1 launched three Stingray drone boats against Enubuj west of Kwajalein Island ahead of the landing there. Each Stingray was an LCVP loaded with 6,000lb of tetrytol, which was remotely directed to explode amongst offshore obstacles to clear a path for incoming landing craft. Enubuj was successfully taken, despite one Stingray sinking 600 yards from shore and the other two suffering engine failures. While scouting the reef and seawall on the western beaches of Kwajalein Island at high tide, four LCVPs from UDT-1 were stopped by the large number of coral-heads 500 yards from shore. Two men stripped off

---

E **UNDERWATER DEMOLITION TEAMS, 1944**

1: UDT-1, Kwajalein Atoll, January 1944
Composed of volunteers from each of the armed services, the first two UDTs were trained to survey the approaches to the beachheads in Kwajalein Atoll while tethered by a safety line to a rubber boat or landing craft. This man wears HBT fatigues; it was soon realized that swimming with less clothing was quicker, safer, and more effective.

2: Special Reconnaissance Detachment, USS *Burrfish*, August 1944
Made up of members from UDT-10 and the OSS Maritime Unit in Hawaii, the Special Reconnaissance Detachment operated from the Balao-class submarine USS *Burrfish* to survey the beaches at Peleliu and Yap in the summer of 1944. This was accomplished, but three swimmers failed to return from a mission off Yap on the night of August 18, 1944. This swimmer is camouflaged with black greasepaint for a nighttime mission, and is holding a USN Mk 2 knife.

3: UDT-3, Leyte, October 1944
UDTs rarely carried small arms on operations and were strongly discouraged from personally engaging the Japanese, to prevent these specialists being needlessly wasted in combat. Those who did bring firearms with them found the .38cal Smith & Wesson Victory revolver ideal, because water drained out of its chamber faster than with a .45cal semiautomatic. Due to the muddy waters churned up by a recent typhoon, UDTs off Leyte found their dive masks to be useless, and conducted their reconnaissance more by touch than by sight.

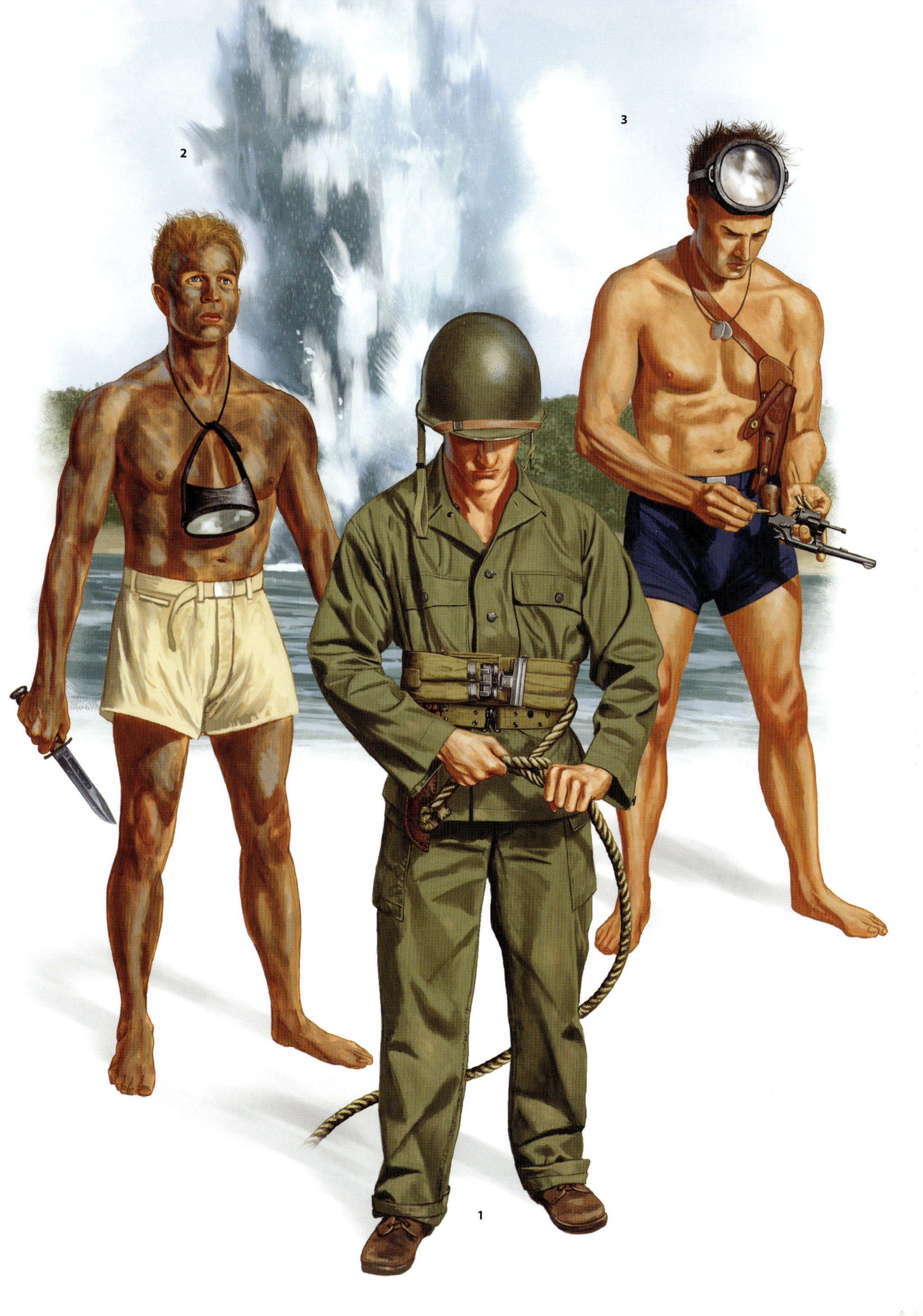
2
3
1

Off Balikpapan, Borneo in June 1945, a swimmer awaits the signal to go over the side of a rubber boat that is being towed alongside a landing craft. The standard of dress in the UDTs during their operations earned them the nickname "the naked warriors." The term "frogmen" was not applied to them until immediately after the war, when the press were finally allowed to chronicle their hitherto secret exploits. (NARA)

their fatigues and dove into the water, noting the coral-heads, water depth, and defensive positions along the beach; based on their report, the following day the landings took place with LVTs. UDT-1 marked coral-heads with buoys, and blew passages through the reef. A few Japanese-manned pillboxes were also demolished with explosives placed alongside them.

On the night of January 31, UDT-2 scouted the southern beaches of Roi-Namur in motor-powered rubber boats while it was being bombarded. Finding the approach deep enough for landing craft and free of obstacles, UDT-2 launched its Stingrays against the outlying reef. The first drone went haywire and had to be boarded and disabled; the second circled back and rammed the LVT serving as its command craft, luckily without exploding. Both Stingrays were then steered out of the way of the incoming Marines. After the landings UDT-2 blasted the edge of the reef for the LSTs to land, and blew up Japanese blockhouses. UDT-1 later supported the landings at Eniwetok Atoll on February 17 by scouting its reef, and ensured the lagoon could accommodate shipping by clearing its channels and moorings with explosives.

With the Marshall Islands secure, UDT-1 and UDT-2 were disbanded and their Army and Marine members were returned to their parent units. It had been decided that future UDTs would be more productive as an all-Navy organization to enhance unit cohesion, and also that swimming to the beach to survey the approaches would be more effective than wading in tethered to a boat. The remaining cadre of demolitioneers became the nucleus of new UDTs at the Naval Combat Demolition Training & Experimental Base, established alongside the Kamaole Amphibious Training Base on Maui in Hawaii in March 1944. UDTs that were formed here were composed of Fort Pierce graduates and later of volunteers from the Pacific Fleet.

The minimal value of the Stingray boats had become evident when the Kwajalein landings succeeded without them; the drones had in fact been doomed to failure by the decisions to use salvaged landing craft that could barely stay afloat, and not to bother with waterproofing the control mechanism. Thereafter their use in the Pacific was discontinued in favor of the more effective method of demolishing obstacles with hand-placed charges.

Saipan

On the morning of June 14, 1944, LCP(R)s dropped swimmers from UDT-5 north of Susupe Point, 500–600 yards from the offshore reef that extended 1,800 yards from Saipan's western beaches. Although naval gunfire kept Japanese mortar fire to a minimum, some swimmers committed their survey data to memory to avoid becoming targets if they paused to write on their Plexiglas plates. UDT-5 also used 11 "surfboards" to direct operations, each with an enlisted man and an officer. Unfortunately, when the naval gunfire subsided to allow for the expected close air support, this never materialized. Rifle, mortar, and machine-gun fire from the beach rained down on the UDTs, hitting four surfboards and sinking one; one swimmer was killed and concussions from shell-bursts injured several others. With the survey completed, the swimmers swam underwater as much as possible to the pickup point, where many of the LCP(R)s had to stop to pull exhausted swimmers out the water.

Meanwhile, UDT-7 surveyed the beaches south of Susupe Point, including the channel through the reef in front of the small town of Charan Kanoa. Despite covering fire from ships offshore, a mortar bomb exploded under the bow of one LCP(R), while another was so riddled with machine-gun bullets that it did not drop its swimmers into the water. While waiting for its swimmers to return, another LCP(R) was hit by a mortar, killing one and wounding two of the crew. Six swimmers surveyed the lagoon to within 50–100 yards of the beach, before withdrawing under a smokescreen as Japanese fire prematurely revealed the mortars and machine guns aboard a dozen barges moored off Charan Kanoa. The reconnaissance swim uncovered no underwater obstacles, but revealed that the lagoon at the northernmost part of the landing beaches was too deep to allow for tanks to land there as originally planned. When the landings commenced on June 15, two LVTs with swimmers aboard led the tanks to a suitable beach along a diagonal route just north of Susupe Point while under mortar fire. That night, off Marpi Point on the northern coast, the APD USS *Gilmer* with UDT-5 aboard sank four Japanese boats carrying reinforcements.

As swimmers left one side of their landing craft, their floating satchel charges were tossed overboard on the other side. Despite their close proximity here, swimmers were normally dropped off at least 100 yards apart to reduce the risk of heavy casualties from a single shell-burst. (NARA)

Guam

On the afternoon of July 14, 1944, UDT-3 conducted a reconnaissance swim off Asan, where they discovered that the offshore reef which extended 200–350 yards from the shore had been covered with rock-filled wire crib obstacles. Later that night, four LCP(R)s dropped off eight LCR(S)s 300 yards off the beach, each carrying a six-man team. While one man stayed with the boat with an SCR-536 radio and a red light to signal the LCP(R), the others crawled along the tide-exposed reef taking note of man-made obstructions, up to only 50 yards from where the Japanese were busy installing more obstacles. Machine-gun fire sank one LCR(S), but its crew was rescued the next morning.

During the days before the landing, UDTs conducted several reconnaissance feints along the coast to tempt Japanese positions into revealing themselves. UDT-3 and UDT-4 then conducted a survey under heavy fire of the reef off Agat beach, where they found 200–300 yards covered with rock-filled log cribs and barbed-wire posts. On the night of July 17, UDT-3 and UDT-4 went in with LCR(S)s, and over a period of two hours they cleared the obstacles off the reefs in front of the Asan and Agat landing beaches with explosives. Several gaps were blown that night, with the remaining obstacles demolished over the next two days. Ships offshore continued to knock out artillery and mortar positions that fired on the UDTs. On the day before the landings UDT-4 placed buoys to mark the approaches to the shoreline, while four of its swimmers secretly placed a 'Welcome' sign on the beach for the Marines. UDT-6, meanwhile, did not locate any mines that night on the beaches near Asan. During the landings on July 21, a Japanese sniper killed one swimmer who was standing on the reef near Agat guiding landing craft toward a channel.

With their swimmers in the water off Balikpapan in June 1945, the crew of an LCP(R) remain vigilant in case immediate support is needed. The radioman can summon gunfire from their APD or from other warships offshore if necessary. Note the USAAF-issue flak vests worn by the .30cal machine-gunners in the bow tubs. (NARA)

Tinian

Knowing that a landing on the heavily fortified beaches in front of Tinian Town on the southwest corner of the island would incur heavy casualties, invasion planners searched for an alternative beachhead. On the evening of July 10, 1944, personnel from UDT-7, along with some Recon Marines, found Asiga Bay in the northeast to be too well fortified for a landing there. On the same night, an attempt by UDT-5 and the Recon Marines to check the small White One and White Two beaches in the northwest was hindered by a northern current that prevented the survey of White Two; but several swimmers explored the 60-yard-long White One beach while the Recon Marines moved inland to reconnoiter its exits. A more successful survey the next night found both beaches suitable for LVTs. On July 23, UDTs swam in front of Tinian Town as part of a feint as it was leveled by air and sea bombardment. UDT-5's attempt to smooth the edge of the reef in front of White One and Two later that night was foiled when rain squalls and rough water forced them to jettison their explosives. A few hours later on July 24, the Marines surprised the Japanese with their landings there, and secured Tinian with light casualties.

Peleliu

In preparation for the landings on Peleliu and Yap, five men from UDT-10 along with five from the OSS MU volunteered to form the Special Reconnaissance Detachment. They were to scout the beaches from rubber boats deployed from the USS *Burrfish*, in the only wartime UDT mission to be launched from a submarine. While evading radar-directed Japanese air and sea patrols the *Burrfish* took photographs of Peleliu's coast, and

On September 14, 1944 off Peleliu, the destroyer USS *Robinson* pours 40mm fire along the shoreline to discourage interference with a UDT which can just be seen as its members work to place explosives on submerged obstacles just beyond the white breaking waves. As well as keeping UDT casualties low, naval gunfire support induced the Japanese to reveal their concealed defensive positions prematurely. (NARA)

43

In contrast to their steel and concrete counterparts in Europe, beach obstacles in the Pacific – such as this one photographed on Peleliu – were primarily made from logs, volcanic rock, and other natural materials. (National UDT-SEAL Museum)

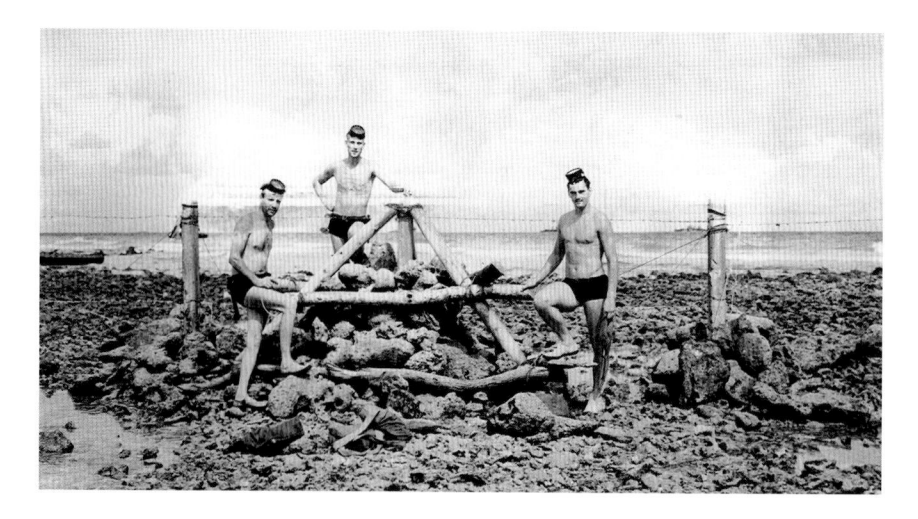

on the night of August 11, 1944 the submarine landed five men to scout its beaches. The submarine then sailed east toward Yap, where another five-man team scouted its reef on the night of August 16. Two nights later a second five-man team went in to scout the reef at Gagil-Tomil on the eastern coast of Yap; two men stayed with the rubber boat while the others swam in toward shore, but the latter were never seen again. Despite a search by the *Burrfish* the fate of these three men remains a mystery.

The following month, swimmers from UDT-6 and UDT-7 scouted Peleliu's western beaches as their LCP(R)s called in naval gunfire on Japanese pillboxes. UDT-7 discovered a double row of wooden posts 75 yards out from shore, with a greater concentration of various obstacles further inshore on the northern half of the landing beaches. On the southern half, UDT-6 discovered a reef strewn with coral boulders and covered with posts, wire fences, and large sawhorse-shaped obstacles made with coconut-tree logs and barbed wire. For two days, starting on the morning of September 13, UDT-6 blasted two paths through the obstacles toward the beach, while ships fired over their heads to discourage snipers. UDT-7 blasted the posts off the reef the night before the Marines landed on September 15. To the north, the Japanese were sending reinforcements to Peleliu from the small island of Ngesebus. Teams from UDT-6 and UDT-7 swam the passage between the two islands on September 27, and found several shallow paths across the 600-yard channel for Marine tanks to ford and seize Ngesebus. Six miles to the southwest, UDT-8 and UDT-10 scouted and demolished obstacles along the landing beaches on Angaur, before the latter team supported the unopposed seizure of Ulithi Atoll. With the timetable for the liberation of the Philippines moved up, the invasion of Yap was canceled.

The success of the UDTs thus far resulted in more teams being raised with volunteers from the Pacific Fleet. All the UDTs were also organized into a separate group under a single commander, whose sole job was to make sure they were prepared and available for upcoming amphibious operations. The group commander was also in charge of the APDs and the ships assigned to provide fire support to the UDTs, and coordinated the operations of his group with the other elements of the amphibious assault. This new command was in place by November 1944, under Capt B. Hall Hanlon with LtCdr Kauffman as his chief of staff.

The Philippines

UDT-3, UDT-4, UDT-5, and UDT-8 surveyed the southern landing areas near Dulag on Leyte on October 18, 1944. This mission was complicated by an earlier typhoon that delayed minesweeping operations, and forced the support ships to stay further out from the coast to avoid any missed mines. With most of the beach defenses untouched by naval gunfire, many LCP(R)s were forced to turn back by small-arms, machine-gun, and mortar fire. They dropped their swimmers for a second attempt, but one LCP(R) from UDT-4 was hit and sunk. Several swimmers were killed or wounded by mortar and sniper fire despite LCP(R) machine-gunners providing covering fire. APDs moved in closer to the beach to bring their 3in guns to bear, which resulted in one Japanese 75mm shell hitting the USS *Goldsborough* and killing and wounding several crewmen. The mud churned up in the water by the typhoon made it difficult for swimmers to conduct their reconnaissance, but no mines or obstacles were found. UDT-6, UDT-9, and UDT-10 faced the same challenges the following day while surveying the northern beaches along San Pedro Bay near Tacloban. Again, they failed to locate any mines or obstacles, and UDT-6 and UDT-9 each had one LCP(R) sunk by Japanese fire. During the landings on October 20 a few LSTs got stuck on a sandbar hidden by the muddy water.

As the US fleet arrived off Lingayen Gulf in Luzon on January 7, 1945, UDT-5, UDT-9, and UDT-15 surveyed the southern beaches in front of Lingayen Town, while UDT-8, UDT-10, and UDT-14 covered the eastern beaches at San Fabian. Along with the standard naval gunfire support, two LCI(G)s assigned to each team provided them with 20mm and 40mm covering fire. Little enemy fire was sustained, and the swimmers discovered a few sandbars but no mines or obstacles. On the day after the landings on January 10, UDT-5 and UDT-15 surveyed other sites for LSTs to unload their cargo. On January 12 a kamikaze crashed into the APD USS *Belknap*, killing 38 men of whom 11 were from UDT-9. Early on the morning of January 29, UDT-10 surveyed the beach at Zambales ahead of a landing there to cut off the Bataan Peninsula from the retreating Japanese. After locating several sandbars the swimmers were greeted by Filipino guerrillas, and an unopposed landing followed.

Swimmers were recovered from the water into the rubber boat lashed alongside the landing craft either by grabbing a rubber figure-of-eight snare, or by their teammates hauling them aboard by hand. They would quickly climb across to the landing craft, to make way for the next swimmer. (National UDT-SEAL Museum)

As they speed away from Peleliu, a UDT look back to see 8,000lb of tetrytol instantly clear a beach of obstacles. After the landings UDTs would return to the beach to clear it of obstructions to allow more landing craft to supply the beachhead. (NARA)

Iwo Jima

On February 16, 1945, a group from UDT-13 paddled ashore on Higashi 2 miles off the northeast coast of Iwo Jima to install a navigation beacon, while naval gunfire helped subdue the mortar and machine-gun fire unleashed against the swimmers. The following morning UDT-12, UDT-13, UDT-14, and UDT-15 surveyed the eastern beaches with support provided by carrier planes, destroyers, and LCI(G)s. The Japanese opened fire from hidden artillery batteries, sinking one LCI(G) and severely damaging the others. Balanced against these losses, the LCI(G)s had inadvertently tricked the previously unknown artillery positions into revealing themselves, and they were subsequently knocked out by carrier aircraft and naval gunfire. For their actions LCI(G) Group 8 received the Presidential Unit Citation.

Despite a smokescreen and naval gunfire, swimmers stayed submerged as best they could during their reconnaissance missions in order to avoid the torrent of mortar and small-arms fire. The volcanic sand they gathered from

F — UNDERWATER DEMOLITION TEAMS, 1945

1: UDT-15, Iwo Jima, February 1945

Shown here aboard his LCP(R) while preparing for a reconnaissance swim, this sailor wears an M1 helmet and an N-3 jacket against the cold wind as the landing craft heads for the eastern beaches of Iwo Jima. He carries Churchill swim fins, which he will put on over the canvas "coral shoes" that protect his feet from potentially poisonous cuts when standing on coral reefs. His skin is smeared with aluminum greasepaint in an attempt to insulate him from the chill of the water during the swim; upon his return he will be given long underwear and a ration of brandy to help him warm up. Many swimmers suffered from cramps due to long exposure to the cold winter sea.

2: UDT-21, Ie Shima, June 1945

For the invasion of Ie Shima a few miles west of Okinawa in April 1945, UDT-21 blew a channel through its outlying reef. The team returned two months later to improve the channel as the island was prepared to facilitate the invasion of Japan. This swimmer is checking TNT blocks and primacord for Mk 133 chain demolition charges; the satchel charges will be tossed into the water and connected up by primacord with explosives already laid in the channel. His blue sweater will provide added warmth in the cold water.

3: UDT-18, Balikpapan, June 1945

In the last UDT combat operation of the war, this swimmer is completely submerged to avoid being spotted by the Japanese as he swims toward the beach to conduct his offshore survey. Although his Plexiglas slate and waterproof pencil are hung around his neck for easy access, some swimmers simply committed information to memory to avoid staying in one place any longer than necessary. He wears his Churchill swim fins over canvas "coral shoes."

1
2
3
BLOCK DEMOLITION CHAIN M1
BLOCK DEMOLITION CHAIN M1
TNT
RECTANGULAR
BLOCKS,
DEMOLITION,
IN 2 HAVERSACKS
DUPONT

below the water line (in tobacco pouches) turned out not to be representative of the sand on the island itself, which was of a far looser composition and would play havoc with vehicles during the battle. No obstacles were found, and the few anti-boat mines that were discovered were successfully destroyed. Two swimmers from UDT-12 placed a navigation beacon on Futatsu Rock 300 yards from the beach. Many of the swimmers suffered from cramps in the 65°F water as the offshore current swept many of them north, to where LCP(R)s from different UDTs recovered them. One swimmer from UDT-12 was killed by mortar fire, while a sniper killed an LCP(R) crewman from UDT-15. That afternoon the UDTs successfully surveyed the alternative landing beaches on the western side of Iwo Jima without loss. On the night of February 18, a bomb from a Japanese aircraft hit the APD USS *Blessman* while it was on picket duty; of the 38 men killed, 18 were from UDT-15. For days following the assault landing UDTs helped clear the beachhead of over 200 wrecked landing craft. After several demolitions on the beach created a prohibitive amount of shrapnel, the wrecks were dragged back into the water before being sunk with explosives. Only UDT-12 received the Presidential Unit Citation for its role at Iwo Jima.

Okinawa

Two groups of UDTs supported the invasion of Okinawa; Underwater Demolition Group Able had UDT-12, UDT-13, UDT-14, and UDT-19, while Group Baker was composed of UDT-4, UDT-7, UDT-11, UDT-16, UDT-17, and UDT-21.

On March 25, 1945, Group Able scouted eight separate beaches in the Kerama Islands southwest of Okinawa. Naval gunfire subdued Japanese defensive fire while the swimmers determined that the 77th Infantry Division could land the next day in landing craft, except for two western islands that could only be reached with LVTs. Next to be surveyed were the Keise Shima Islands just off the western coast, where Japanese soldiers surprised a small party from UDT-19 on Kamiyama. While one swimmer covered them with pistol and carbine fire, the party retreated to their rubber boat and withdrew from the island, with only one man wounded.

On March 29, with naval bombardment keeping Japanese fire to a minimum, Group Baker noted the numerous wooden posts that covered the outlying reef on the western coast of Okinawa. Meanwhile UDT-12 and UDT-14 conducted a survey of beaches on the southeastern coast, and the next day they placed explosives along its reef to help deceive the Japanese into expecting a landing there. On March 30, Group Baker placed explosives amongst the wooden posts on the western reef, with the morning tide providing an effective cover. All of the posts were successfully demolished except for those assigned to UDT-16. As a "fleet team" made up of volunteers from the Pacific Fleet, and considered by the other UDTs to be less well trained, UDT-16 was unfairly maligned and denied the opportunity to finish the job, which was completed by UDT-11 the next morning; it was later suspected that waves had severed the main trunk line from the explosives UDT-16 had placed on the obstacles.

While scouting Nakagusuku Bay on April 9, the APD USS *Hopping* eliminated a Japanese shore battery but was itself hit by several shells, killing one man and wounding eight from UDT-7. Offshore, the APDs helped fight off kamikaze attacks and assisted nearby ships struck by them. However, the APD USS *Bates* was sunk off Ie Shima on May 25, forcing UDT-12 to transfer to another APD, the USS *Amesbury*. Subsequently, as the US Tenth Army advanced south, the UDTs surveyed beaches close to the frontlines and on offshore islands to assist supply efforts.

Borneo

On June 8, 1945, UDT-11 and its support ships sailed through 20 miles of an uncharted minefield to within half a mile of Labuan Island in Brunei Bay, where they surveyed the coast while under Japanese mortar and machine-gun fire. No obstacles were found, but one swimmer was killed and six injured by bombs accidentally dropped by USAAF aircraft. On June 25, UDT-11 was joined by UDT-18 to reconnoiter the shoreline north of Balikpapan, which proved to be covered by a solid wall of wooden obstacles, cables, and mines 50 yards from the beach. Offshore mines kept the support ships at a distance, while smoke from burning oil fires obscured some of the beaches. The UDTs returned the next day to blow two 800-yard gaps through the obstacles, with little opposition. On June 27 they surveyed the beaches at Balikpapan, which were covered by rain and oil-smoke. Despite the bombardment by low-flying US bombers, heavy shellfire landed near the swimmers, giving one a concussion. Next day the UDTs placed their explosives along the thick wall of obstacles while coming under heavy mortar fire that hit several landing craft. Naval and aerial bombardment subdued this fire, but one gap was blown prematurely after a Japanese shell set off the explosives UDT-11 had placed. Those set by UDT-18 blew another gap as planned. On June 30, UDT-11 blew the remaining obstacles between the two gaps to aid the Australian landing the following day. For its actions off Okinawa, Brunei Bay, and Balikpapan, UDT-11 was awarded the Presidential Unit Citation.

In the weeks following the surrender of Japan, UDTs assisted in its demilitarization by demolishing stockpiles of weapons and munitions. Here two men from UDT-18 attach explosives to the tail of a midget submarine. (National UDT-SEAL Museum)

The Japanese surrender

About 28 UDTs had been scheduled to participate in the invasion of mainland Japan, but the two atomic bombs dropped in August 1945 abruptly changed their mission from invasion to one of occupation. Eighteen UDTs were quickly sent by plane or ship to rendezvous with forces about to land in Japan, China, and Korea. UDT-21 became the first naval personnel to land in Japan, on August 29 on the Futsusaki peninsula, where it left a 'Welcome' sign for the Marines before searching for mines at the mouth of Tokyo Bay. UDTs prepared docks and beaches for the arrival of occupation forces, and neutralized any coastal defenses and ships they encountered. For several weeks after the surrender the Japanese assisted the UDTs in locating and destroying suicide boats, midget submarines, and various naval ordnance along the coast.

NAVAL GROUP CHINA

In February 1942 the Commander-in-Chief of the US Fleet, Adm Ernest King, secretly ordered Cdr Milton Miles to China as part of a long-term plan to support US Navy operations in the Pacific, officially known as the Friendship Project. Miles was to set up weather stations, mine coastal areas and rivers, prepare the coastline for a possible American landing in the future, and harass the Japanese at any opportunity.

Commander Miles had previously served two tours of duty in China with the US Asiatic Fleet, during which he gained an appreciation of Chinese culture and learned to speak Cantonese and Mandarin. After Miles's arrival in the Chinese Nationalist capital of Chungking in May 1942, his respect for the Chinese and willingness to work with them as equals quickly found favor with Gen Tai Li, who was deeply suspicious of most foreigners. The general was head of the Chinese Bureau of Investigation & Statistics (BIS) – the Nationalist Army's intelligence department. Together they inspected the Chinese coast opposite Formosa, and, while they were taking cover together

The amiability seen here between Gen Tai Li (left) and Capt Milton Miles USN, photographed at "Happy Valley" in December 1942, was genuine. It reflected a shared spirit of respect and cooperation that made SACO a much more effective military organization than some other joint Sino-American efforts during the war. (Courtesy Dr Charles H. Miles)

from a Japanese air raid outside the village of Pucheng, Tai Li asked Miles to train and arm 50,000 of his guerrillas in exchange for allowing US naval activities in China with his support. Understanding that the guerrillas would protect the weather stations and other US Navy operations, Miles agreed.

Tai Li and Miles presented their expanded vision of the collaborative operations to Nationalist president Generalissimo Chiang Kai-shek, who insisted that a formal compact must be agreed and signed between the United States and China. This operation took the name Sino-American Cooperative Organization (SACO), which replaced the Friendship Project. Signed by American and Chinese officials in Washington, DC in April 1943, this stipulated that the US Navy would train and arm Tai Li's Loyal Patriotic Army and other aligned guerrilla groups, and supply the equipment needed to establish weather, coast-watching and radio stations in China. The BIS would provide personnel, transport, facilities, and intelligence gathered from its network of agents. Tai Li was made director, with Miles as his deputy; Miles was made a lieutenant general in the Nationalist Chinese Army and, in the normal course of his service, was promoted to captain in the US Navy. SACO became a naval contingent, in which more than 2,000 Americans would serve by the end of the war, alongside 97,000 Chinese guerrillas, 20,000 independent operators, and thousands of Chinese policemen in Japanese-occupied China.

"Happy Valley"

As the first naval personnel of the Friendship Project arrived in September 1942, their main headquarters was set up in a secluded valley 8 miles northwest of Chungking that became known as "Happy Valley." Throughout the war this served as the main administrative hub for SACO, with separate departments for personnel, intelligence, operations, supply, communications, radio interception, and aerology. Newly arrived Americans were instructed in proper behavior toward the Chinese, with an emphasis on cooperation and respect for their culture. This included making efforts to learn their language, eating their food, and sharing their hardships. Happy Valley also served as a training area for courses in hand-to-hand combat, demolitions, medicine, radio, aerology, and photography. On the other side of a nearby mountain a satellite training camp was established, to teach criminal investigation techniques to BIS officers in order to improve their police and counterintelligence skills. The instructors were Americans from the naval contingent who had served in law enforcement before the war.

Chosen for its agreeable climate and sufficient water supply, "Happy Valley" served as the main SACO headquarters from October 1942. Chinese and American officers and enlisted men ate local food side-by-side in the mess hall located in the center of the valley. (Courtesy Dr Charles H. Miles)

Along with transmitting weather reports and intelligence each day, Fleet Radio Unit China intercepted and broke Japanese military codes. In May 1944 and June 1945 it tracked planes carrying Japanese admirals, which were then intercepted and shot down by US 14th Air Force units. (Courtesy Dr Charles H. Miles)

Happy Valley maintained constant contact with SACO units in the field, and with a Chinese communications net made up of 600 hand-cranked radios whose operators monitored Japanese radio transmissions and reported other intelligence obtained in the field. The radio schedules for each of the field units to send in its reports were strictly set at a specific 30-minute period every second day, to accommodate the limited number of receivers back at Happy Valley (homing pigeons were also used to send back messages). In May 1944, Fleet Radio Unit China was established 20 miles south of Kunming, and that September it began sending weather reports to the Pacific Fleet four times a day. Relevant intelligence reports were also sent to American commands throughout Asia and the Pacific, and directly to Washington, DC when necessary.

Miniature terrain-model "maps," such as this one of Kweilin, were used to plan and coordinate attacks by Chinese guerrillas against Japanese garrisons. (Courtesy Dr Charles H. Miles)

Inter-service rivalries

Despite the SACO Agreement, Capt Miles found himself caught up in a maelstrom of political intrigue involving the US Army, the OSS, and the Nationalist Chinese.

The US Army Chief of Staff, Gen George C. Marshall, initially objected to Miles serving under Tai Li and reporting directly to Adm King instead of to Gen Joseph Stilwell, the US Army commander of the China-Burma-India Theater. The US Army fundamentally believed that the US Navy should not be conducting ground operations anywhere, and that US personnel should not serve under the command of a foreign power. However, Marshall relented when Stilwell expressed his support for the SACO Agreement, since it would guarantee cooperation from Tai Li and greater control over OSS activities in China (which were regarded with suspicion by the Army). In fact Miles enjoyed good relations with Stilwell, who agreed that SACO should receive a monthly supply quota of 150 tons (out of a total of 18,200 tons per month by June 1944) that was flown over "the Hump" from India to China. Nevertheless, ignorance of and indifference toward SACO by the US Army-controlled Air Transport Command often reduced the amount of supplies it received each month.

SACO units had to improvise with local materials, and work around shortages such as the lack of nails, to make equipment operational; this is a radio direction-finder near the Inner Mongolian border. The trousers and fur hats illustrate the harsh climate that personnel based at Camp Four had to endure. (Courtesy Dr Charles H. Miles)

Although he did not help compose it, OSS director William Donovan signed the SACO Agreement as a first step toward his agency operating independently in China. Without consulting him first, Donovan had appointed Miles as Chief of OSS Operations in the Far East in September 1942 as a way to gain a foothold in China. Tai Li learned of the appointment before Miles did, and it caused some friction between them, though this was quickly resolved. Donovan's attempts to undermine Miles's authority nearly jeopardized the entire SACO Agreement; frustrated by the limitations imposed upon the OSS and by the poor quality and quantity of intelligence he felt it was receiving, Donovan personally fired Miles from the OSS in Chungking in December 1943. Both the US Army and the OSS believed that Miles was too accommodating to Tai Li, while Miles countered that having a strong relationship with the Chinese general based on trust and respect was the only way to ensure the success of the US Navy's mission in China. In January 1944 the Joint Chiefs of Staff declared that Donovan did not have the authority to dismiss Miles from the OSS. Attempts to reach an accommodation between SACO and the OSS quickly reached an impasse, and both organizations operated separately from each other in China. Captain Miles was promoted to commodore that March, and despite the difficulties he encountered Adm King maintained his strong support. The naval contingent of SACO was designated as Naval Group China in mid-1944.

General Albert Wedemeyer replaced Gen Stilwell in October 1944, and in April 1945 he attempted to amend the SACO Agreement to place the personnel and material of Naval Group China under his authority, though Chinese opposition prevented him from gaining control of its operations. Wedemeyer then issued an illegal order that gave him control over Naval Group China; he immediately denied it reinforcements (though allowing replacements), delayed new operations, and conducted numerous investigations into its actions. Soon afterward, training programs ceased due to neglect and mismanagement. The limitations on manpower were not lifted until July 1945, after a visiting congressman threatened Wedemeyer that he would inform the President about the hundreds of naval personnel who had been lingering in camps in India for several months. In the event only a small number of them entered China before the war ended.

G: NAVAL GROUP CHINA

1: Small-arms instructor; Camp Three, Honan Province, November 1943

Americans in SACO trained Chinese guerrillas in the use of small arms such as this UD42 Marlin submachine gun. Ammunition for it was plentiful, due to the large stocks of 9mm cartridges that the Germans shipped to China when advising its army before World War II. Other small arms supplied and trained on included the .38cal Smith & Wesson revolver, .45cal M1911A1 semiautomatic pistol, .30cal M1 carbine, .45cal M1 Thompson SMG, .30cal M1903 Springfield rifle, .30cal Lewis machine gun, and 2.36in M1 bazooka.

2: Weather observer, Unit Four; Suiyan Province, February 1945

Northernmost and most strategically important of the weather stations set up by SACO, Camp Four (later Unit Four) was located at the southern edge of the Gobi Desert. The Americans who served there found locally made sheepskin parkas better able to protect them from the winter temperatures (which dropped to -30°F) than this US Navy-issued cold weather gear, and acquired local fur hats. They too armed and trained Chinese guerrillas, who on May 14, 1945 turned back a Japanese armored detachment after a three-hour battle 130 miles east of the weather station.

3: Coast-watcher, Unit Six; Fukien Province, November 1944

Americans who served as coast-watchers also trained Chinese guerrillas not only with small arms, but also in ship and aircraft recognition, chart-reading, and the use of radios, to help them identify and report Japanese movements off the southern Chinese coast. Groups of coast-watchers deliberately kept their numbers down to between five and a dozen men each so as to maintain mobility to help them evade Japanese patrols. Seen here scanning the horizon, this coast-watcher maintains his naval identity with his dark blue deck jacket worn over US Army-issue khaki shirt and trousers.

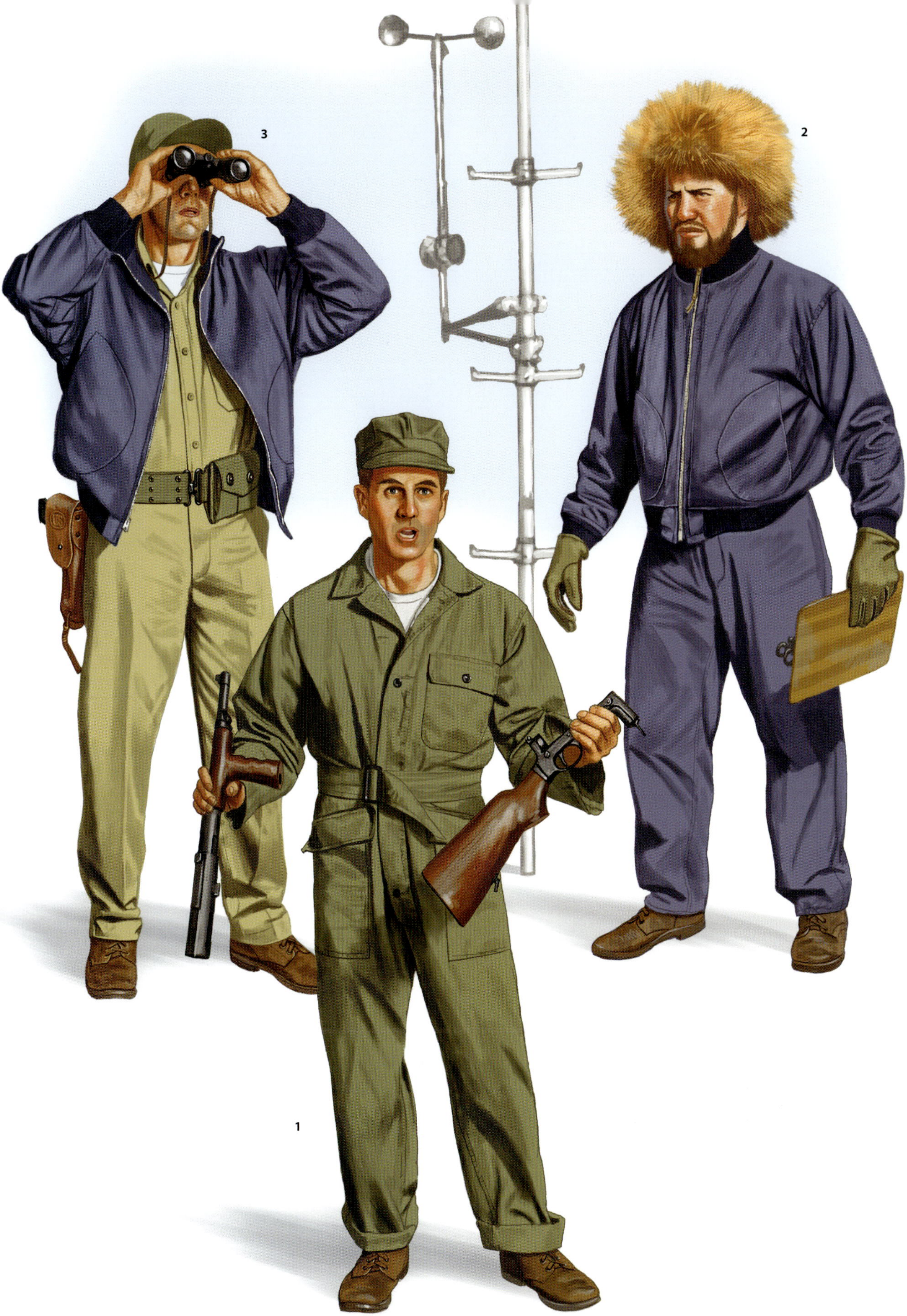
3
2
1

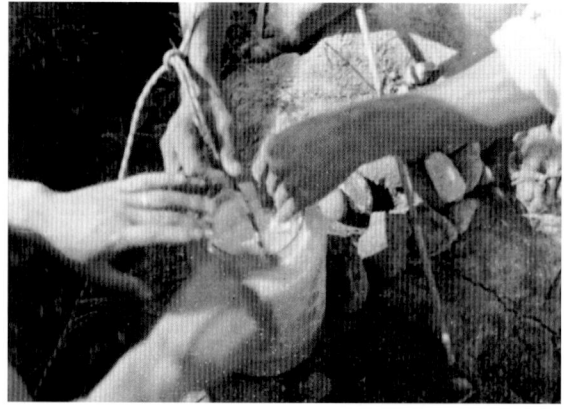

ABOVE
Chinese students listen intently as they are instructed on how to construct booby traps from locally found items. Illustrations like those seen on the table were effective teaching tools, bridging the language barrier. (NARA)

RIGHT
The Japanese *Ichi-Go* offensive in Hunan and Kiangsi provinces in the spring and summer of 1944 seized much Nationalist territory and threatened USAAF air bases. To help defend Changsha, Lt Joseph Champe of the Yangtze Naval Unit bought every glass candy jar he could find locally and filled them with explosives, bits of metal, and sharp rocks before burying them in the roads that led into the city. Detonated remotely by means of the bell-ringer circuits from old field telephones, these improvised mines inflicted severe casualties before Changsha fell in July. (Courtesy Dr Charles H. Miles)

Navy/Air Force cooperation

Miles had a good working relationship with USAAF Gen Claire Chennault's 14th Air Force, which began in October 1942 with the establishment of a liaison group that eventually became known as the 14th Naval Unit. Along with weather reports, this provided intelligence on Japanese targets through radio interception, photograph interpretation, and field reports. The Shipping Center of the 14th Naval Unit gathered information on the routes, cargoes, and sailing dates of Japanese ships for the 14th AF to bomb. The unit's homemade radio direction-finders also uncovered Japanese-recruited agents who were reporting the flight paths of 14th AF planes from Kunming, and it coordinated efforts with Chinese guerrillas to rescue downed aircrew (76 of them by the war's end). SACO teams also located targets in the field, and occasionally guided in 14th AF planes by radio or white muslin arrows placed on the ground. This coordinated activity increased dramatically in the summer of 1944, as 14th AF planes inflicted heavy casualties and damage upon the Japanese *Ichi-Go* offensive that eventually overran several of its airfields. The 14th AF reciprocated this cooperation when its planes dropped mail and supplies to scattered SACO units throughout China.

OPERATIONS

Guerrilla training and operations

In April 1943, SACO began setting up camps (later known as "units" when Naval Group China was established) to train Chinese guerrillas in small arms, demolition, sabotage, combat techniques, radio handling, aircraft and ship recognition, and aerology. The locations of these camps throughout China were chosen jointly by Miles and Tai Li. About a dozen camps were set up behind or close to Japanese lines where the guerrillas operated, and served as their headquarters. Access to them involved long, arduous journeys over great distances along rivers, poor roads, and simple footpaths. Since resupplying the camps was dubious at best, SACO personnel brought with them from the start all the supplies they would need. Bare necessities such as food and clothing were obtained locally; mail arrived sporadically, if it all. Late in the war, US Navy bombers from the Philippines and Okinawa airdropped supplies to SACO units in the field in exchange for intelligence on targets to attack. In July 1945, US Navy planes began to drop 3,000lb of supplies a day to Changchow and Foochow near the southwestern coast of China after their liberation by Chinese guerrillas.

Instructors on the range supervise Chinese students firing M1 carbines in the prone position; in the left background others can be seen being trained in pistol shooting. American instructors used Chinese phrases that they had picked up, along with hand gestures, facial expressions, and demonstrations to train the guerrillas, who were issued weapons after the completion of their training. (NARA)

Each camp was run by either a US Navy lieutenant or lieutenant commander, or a US Marine Corps major or captain. All the Americans in the camps served as instructors. Miles specifically requested personnel who had some relevant skills that they could teach, and these often went beyond the military specialty they were originally trained for. The Americans were all watched over and protected from potential harm, often without their knowledge, by Tai Li's men. Although some of the recruits the Chinese provided were unhealthy to some degree, they surprised their instructors with their willingness and ability to learn. Initially other Nationalist Chinese generals did not trust the Americans, and were reluctant to work with them until Tai Li forcibly insisted that they do so. Miles worked hard to ensure that cultural differences did not jeopardize cooperation between Americans and Chinese, and mutual trust and respect overcame most differences that came up.

As soon as they were trained, SACO guerrillas began raiding Japanese supply depots and airfields, ambushing columns and junks, derailing trains, and demolishing bridges. Tai Li's vast intelligence network aided their efforts in locating targets to attack. Since the Japanese only had enough troops to occupy cities, towns, and other strategic areas the guerrillas could travel freely across the countryside, and place isolated caches of weapons throughout their areas of operations. Although a few camps were forced to relocate by the Japanese *Ichi-Go* offensive in the spring and summer of 1944, other SACO units took advantage of the chaos to establish training camps further behind Japanese lines.

The Chinese porters who carried SACO supplies and equipment for the establishment of guerrilla camps were local villagers. Hired for a day, they could carry up to a 50lb load at each end of their shoulder-pole while moving at a fast pace, before being relieved by a group from another village further along the trail. (Courtesy Dr Charles H. Miles)

In the spring of 1945, SACO guerrillas began attacking inshore targets and offshore islands alike. On April 16 guerrillas landed on the island of Ockseu, wiped out its small garrison, and demolished the lighthouse and radio station. The following night Upper Seu Island was raided, its installations destroyed and intelligence material retrieved. An operation against the island of Wu Su in July was aborted when heavy Japanese fire prevented the guerrillas from landing.

Chinese-uniformed Americans from Unit Two and Chinese guerrillas from Column Four display captured weapons and equipment after ambushing a Japanese unit in Hunan Province in December 1944. (Courtesy Dr Charles H. Miles)

Japanese shipping was also targeted, as homemade sea mines made out of oil drums half-filled with TNT were placed along the coastal shipping routes north of Amoy. On the night of May 6, Ens John N. Mattmiller and three Chinese swimmers he had personally chosen and trained swam from a nearby sampan and attached homemade limpet mines to the hull of a Japanese freighter in Amoy Harbor; the resulting explosions caused the vessel to roll over onto its side.

Unable to withdraw their garrisons on the islands of Amoy and Quemoy by sea, in late June 1945 the Japanese were forced to march them inland to Swatow, 120 miles to the southwest. Throughout their three-week march the 3,700 Japanese soldiers were constantly ambushed and delayed by SACO guerrillas and soldiers of the Chinese 75th Division. Americans operating with the guerrillas guided in US Navy bombers from the Philippines and Okinawa by radio. As he received reports of the ongoing battle, Gen Tai Li

H: NAVAL GROUP CHINA

1: Guerrilla instructor, Unit Two, winter clothing; Kweichow Province, December 1944

Unit Two was considered the most productive instruction unit in SACO due to the fighting prowess of the guerrillas it trained, and the fact that it could easily be supplied by air and truck. It constantly harassed the advancing Japanese with ambushes and sabotage during their *Ichi-Go* offensive. The Japanese soon learned to dread the guerrillas, nicknaming them "short guns" for the M1 carbines with which they were armed. This American accompanying the guerrillas on an operation wears American web gear over light gray Chinese Army winter uniform, complete with the Kuomintang cap badge.

2: Guerrilla instructor, Unit Five, hot-weather clothing; Kwangsi Province, May 1945

Unit Five operated near the border between southern China and French Indochina in the last full year of the war. Despite being forced by the Japanese to move northwest from its original base at Nanning in November 1944, Unit Five and the columns it supported continued to carry out ambushes and attacks on installations, finally helping to liberate Nanning the following May. Some histories state that Americans in SACO only wore khaki clothing, but available photographs show that a wide variety of US Navy garments were worn in the field.

3: Submachine-gunner, Yangtze Naval Unit; Kiangsi Province, June 1945

Operating in central China between the Tungting and Poyang lakes, the Yangtze Naval Unit disrupted Japanese supply lines along the Hankow–Canton railroad and the Yangtze river. Beginning in August 1944, they derailed trains, ambushed truck convoys, demolished bridges, cut telephone lines, and attacked warehouses, radio stations, and other key installations. Along the Yangtze they sank ships with improvised mines, and spotted other river traffic for the 14th Air Force. They were the only unit in SACO that was recommended for the Navy Unit Citation.

4: SACO "What the Hell?" pennant

The personal pennant of Milton Miles, flown at "Happy Valley" and throughout China during the war. As the XO of the destroyer USS *Wickes* in 1934, Lt Miles had it made up so as to request, in his unique way, a clarification of unclear orders during naval maneuvers. During the Japanese invasion of Hainan Island in February 1939, while captain of the destroyer USS *John D. Edwards*, Miles used it to confuse Japanese ships long enough to allow his warship to anchor offshore to check on the wellbeing of Americans on the island. When confronted by a Japanese admiral about the exact meaning of the pennant, Miles responded that the Imperial Japanese Navy needed to keep their signal books up to date....

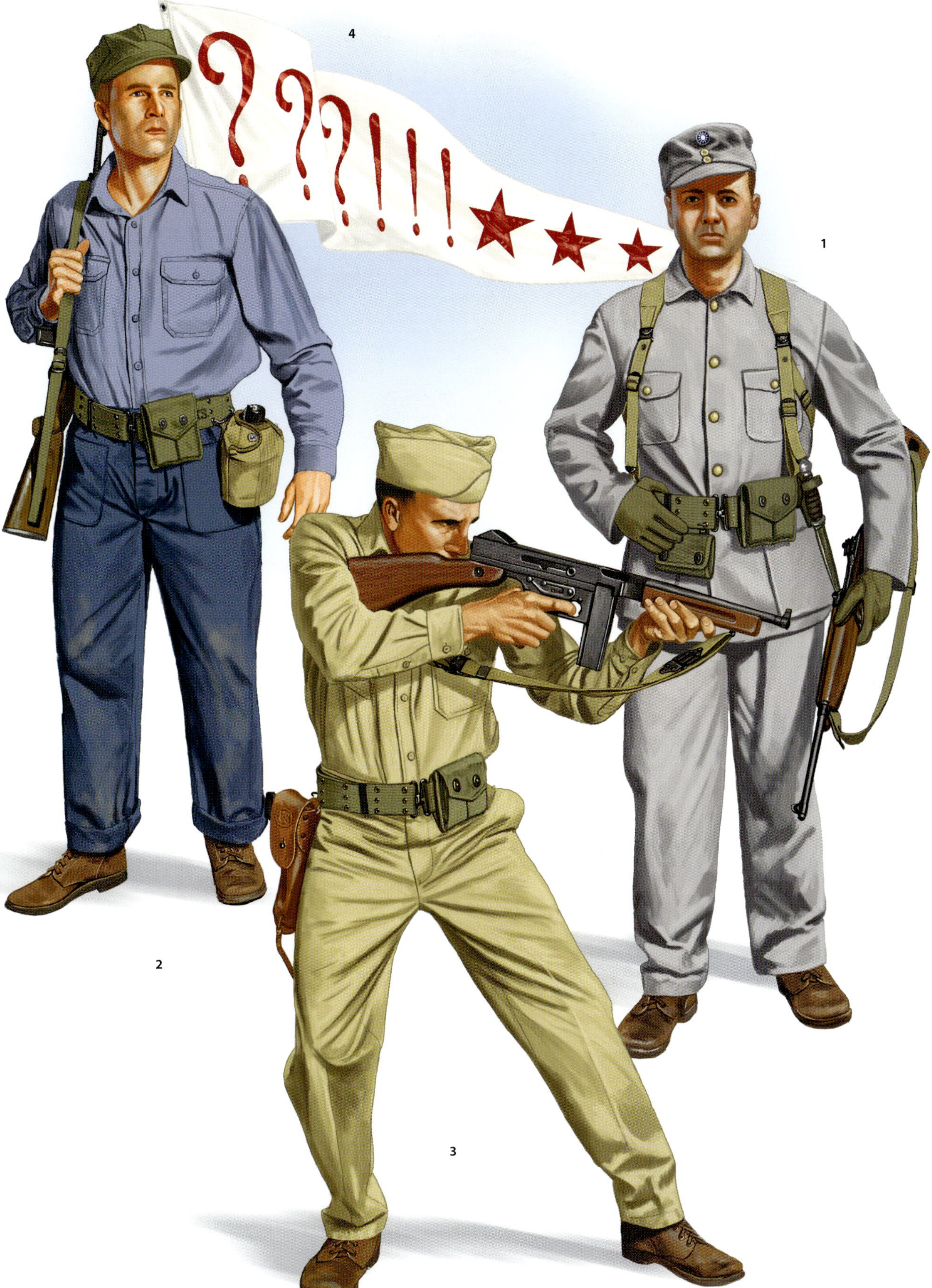

4
??!!!★★★
1
2
3

expressed his satisfaction that the Chinese were fighting like Americans, acting independently and decisively without relying on orders from higher headquarters. The Japanese suffered at least 1,500 casualties from the SACO assaults (they burned most of their dead, making an accurate count difficult to determine).

Although US amphibious landings along the Chinese coast never took place, over 80 percent of potential landing sites had been surveyed by July 1945. When the war ended SACO controlled the ports at Amoy, Changchow, and Foochow, and the airfields at Changchow and Foochow. Almost 600 miles of coastline between Swatow and Hangchow was also under SACO control. In total, the guerrillas trained and supported by SACO/Naval Group China had destroyed more than 200 bridges, 84 locomotives, and 141 ships and river craft. Their activities were responsible for the deaths of around 71,000 Japanese military personnel, and the guerrillas themselves killed about 30,000 – a rate of 2½ Japanese for each weapon supplied to the guerrillas by SACO. This "kill ratio" was unmatched by any branch of the American military during the war.

Pact Doc

Medical treatment for Chinese guerrillas was poor to non-existent before US Navy doctors and pharmacist's mates assigned to SACO reached the field. A medical center was set up in June 1943 at Tung An in Hunan Province, but this was too far from the fighting, and many Chinese soldiers died of their wounds before they could reach it. This led to the establishment of the Pact Doc hospital and medical school near Lingling, and the first of 24 medical dispensaries and three mobile field hospitals that were set up behind the lines in November 1943. Staffed by American and Chinese doctors, US Navy pharmacist's mates, and local graduates of Pact Doc, they provided immediate medical care for the guerrillas. Pharmacist's mates also accompanied them in the field, and were cross-trained in guerrilla tactics. The limited amount of medical supplies available was supplemented with improvised equipment made out of scrap metal and bamboo, and bandages were washed and reused. After being forced to relocate to Hweichow in Anhwei Province by the Japanese advance in the summer of 1944, Pact Doc was split into two, with one hospital at Kienow in northeastern Fukien Province and the other near Suian in western Chekiang Province in the spring of 1945.

Weather stations

Weather patterns above the Pacific form first over the Asian interior and travel eastward, which made weather forecasts from the Chinese mainland important for Pacific Fleet operations. In August 1942, two Navy aerographer's mates arrived in Chungking to set up Weather Central at Happy Valley. This team coordinated Chinese weather reports from the Central Meteorological Bureau, Combined Organization of Aviation Affairs, and the Chinese National Aviation Cooperation, together with intercepted Japanese and Russian weather reports. Despite a year of effort, the

A USN pharmacist's mate performs a medical checkup on a Chinese guerrilla at a makeshift Pact Doc dispensary. Such care helped to maintain the strong morale of the guerrillas; downed American fliers, escaped Allied POWs, and local Chinese civilians were also treated. (Courtesy Dr Charles H. Miles)

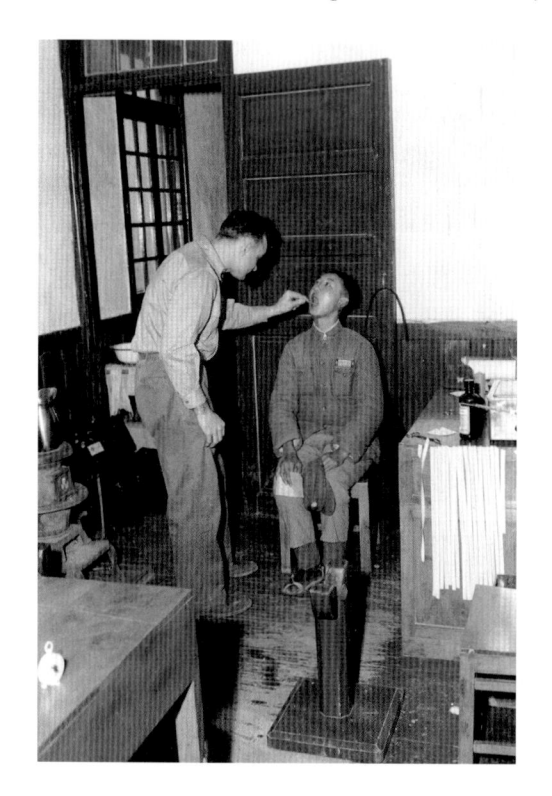

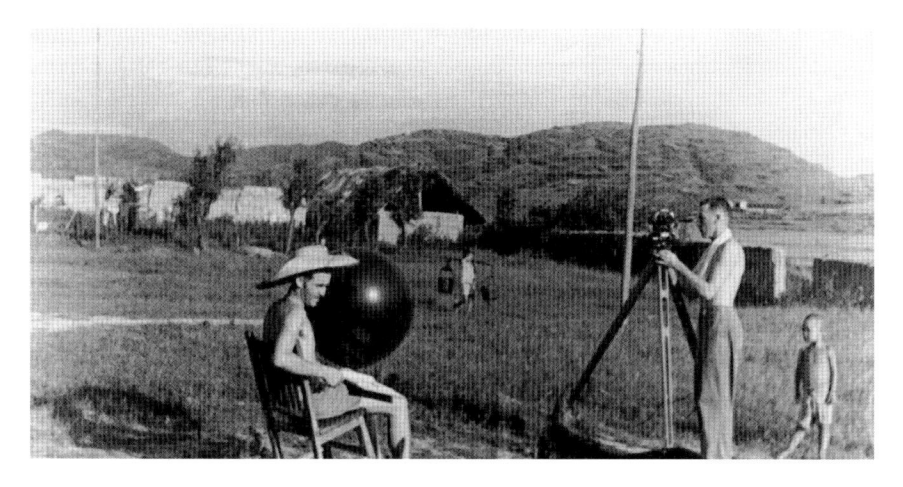

This makeshift weather station in a Chinese village is about to measure the local wind speed and direction. Upon its release the rubber balloon will be observed through the theodolite on the right, and the elevation and azimuth angles of the balloon at specific intervals will be recorded as part of the data reported daily to Weather Central at Happy Valley. (Courtesy Dr Charles H. Miles.)

weather reports were rarely timely or consistent due to the unreliable and overworked Chinese communications net, which saw some reports being delivered by runners several days late. This situation improved when more radios became available.

A separate chain of SACO weather stations, along with its own radio network and code, was soon set up throughout China. As more Chinese recruits were trained on how to accurately gather weather data (many with just barometers and thermometers), they established stations at SACO training camps, coast-watching stations, 14th AF airfields, and other strategic spots in both free and occupied China. American and Chinese radio operators transmitted data to Weather Central up to three times a day. The northernmost site was Camp Four in Suiyan Province near the border with Inner Mongolia. Set up in January 1944, its location in the Gobi Desert allowed it to be the first to detect incoming weather patterns as they passed into China, and its strategic location made it necessary to radio seven reports a day.

A coast-watcher radio station transmits the latest intelligence from a disused temple on Nan Tai mountain; this offered an excellent view of Amoy harbor as well as the nearby island of Quemoy. Coast-watchers never stayed in one place for long, and had to evade Japanese patrols by moving inland into the mountains. American personnel wore Chinese clothing, and yellowed their skin with the anti-malaria drug atabrine and frequent sunbathing to make them less conspicuous. (Courtesy Dr Charles H. Miles)

Coast-watching

Captain Miles set up five SACO coast-watching nets with their own radio networks between Shanghai and Hong Kong. Each of these nets consisted of several small mobile groups dispersed along the coast, who spotted and reported Japanese ship movements for the benefit of US Navy submarines and the 14th Air Force. Chinese pirates were recruited to gather intelligence by trading with the crews of anchored Japanese ships. US Navy carrier planes, along with PB4Y Privateer long-range maritime patrol planes flying in from the Philippines and later Okinawa, were guided in toward targets of opportunity by coast-watchers. Downed aircrew rescued by Chinese pirates and guerrillas would express surprise that the US Navy was able to operate freely along the occupied coast.

Coast-watchers constantly changed their locations to avoid Japanese patrols, especially after transmitting their radio reports. The only US Navy personnel in SACO who were captured during the war were three coast-watchers, who survived their captivity. The coast-watchers played a key role in preventing crucial supplies from reaching Japan.

French Indochina

The first major American involvement in French Indochina began in late 1943, when Miles obtained the help of French Navy Cdr Robert Meynier and his Vietnamese wife Katiou (recently rescued from a German internment camp in France by the British Special Operations Executive) to establish a network of coast-watchers along the Vietnamese coastline. The Meyniers recruited customs officers and lighthouse keepers, as well as French officers and influential Vietnamese government officials, as agents along the coast of northern Indochina. What became known as the Meynier Group provided SACO with intelligence on Japanese ship and aircraft movements, weather, defenses, troop movements, and the status of Allied POWs. The report of a Japanese convoy heading for Haiphong allowed the 14th AF to mine its harbor and block it with a sunken freighter for the remainder of the war. The Meyniers' intelligence also aided Adm William Halsey's carrier strikes along the Indochinese coast in January 1945. However, given the rivalry between Free French leaders, Gen Charles De Gaulle's military mission in Chungking relentlessly impeded the efforts of the Meyniers, who were loyal to Gen Henri Giraud. Vichy French administrators also complicated matters due to their distaste for the Meyniers' affiliation, such as it was, with the Free French. These political handicaps finally forced the Meyniers to leave China in mid-1944, but their intelligence network continued to operate for the rest of the war.

One of the two junks crewed by SACO personnel from Camp Eight sails into Shanghai in late August 1945. Each vessel was armed with a .50cal machine gun, two .30cal Lewis guns, and a bazooka. Their defeat and capture of a Japanese-manned junk was the last US naval action of World War II. (Courtesy Dr Charles H. Miles)

The Japanese surrender

The sudden surrender of Japan resulted in Commodore Miles (who was spot-promoted to rear admiral) instructing all SACO units to proceed east to the Japanese-occupied cities to help re-establish control for the Nationalist Chinese government. This was accomplished with little incident. However, two junks manned by SACO personnel were fired on by a Japanese junk as they sailed to Shanghai on August 20. In what turned out to be the final naval action of the war, the Japanese junk was quickly disabled by a fusillade of machine-gun and bazooka fire before being boarded and captured by a SACO crew. On September 4, RAdm Miles established his headquarters in Shanghai, as SACO helped the Nationalist Chinese reassert control over the city and prepare it to welcome the US Seventh Fleet on September 19, 1945.

SELECT BIBLIOGRAPHY

Bush, Elizabeth K., *America's First Frogman: The Draper Kauffman Story* (Annapolis, MD; Naval Institute Press, 2004)

Dockery, Kevin, *Navy SEALs: A Complete History: From World War II to the Present* (New York; Berkley, 2004)

Dockery, Kevin, *Weapons of the Navy SEALs* (New York; Berkley, 2005)

Dunford, Sue Ann & O'Dell, James Douglas, *More than Scuttlebutt: The US Navy Demolition Men in World War II* (Fairport, NY; Selby Marketing Associates Inc, 2009)

Dwyer, John B., *Seaborne Deception: The History of US Navy Beach Jumpers* (New York; Praeger, 1992)

Dwyer, John B., *Scouts and Raiders: The Navy's First Special Warfare Commandos* (Westport, CT; Praeger, 1993)

Dwyer, John B., *Commandos from the Sea: The History of Amphibious Special Warfare in World War II and the Korean War* (Boulder, CO; Paladin Press, 1998)

Fairbanks Jr., Douglas, *A Hell of a War* (New York; St. Martin's Press, 1993)

Fane, Francis Douglas & Moore, Don, *The Naked Warriors: The Story of the US Navy's Frogmen* (Annapolis, MD; Naval Institute Press, 1995)

Gawne, Jonathan, *Spearheading D-Day: American Special Units of the Normandy Invasion* (Paris; Histoire & Collections, 1998)

Higgins, Edward T., *Webfooted Warriors: A Story of a "Frogman" in the Navy During World War II* (New York; Exposition Press, 1955)

Holt, Thaddeus, *The Deceivers: Allied Military Deception in the Second World War* (New York; Scribner, 2004)

Kush, Linda, *The Rice Paddy Navy: US Sailors Undercover in China: Espionage and Sabotage Behind Japanese Lines During World War II* (New York; Osprey Publishing, 2012)

Mathieson, Greg E. & Gatley, Dave, *United States Special Naval Warfare: US Navy SEALS* (Centreville, VA; NSW Publications, 2012)

Miles, Milton E. & Hawthorne, Daniel, *A Different Kind of War: The Little Known Story of the Combined Guerrilla Forces Created in China by the US Navy and the Chinese during World War II* (Garden City, NY; Doubleday, 1967)

Mishler, Clayton, *Sampan Sailor: A Navy Man's Adventures in WWII China* (Washington, DC; Brassey's, 1994)

O'Dell, James Douglas, *The Water is Never Cold: The Origins of the US Navy's Combat Demolition Units, UDTs, and SEALs* (Washington, DC; Brassey's, 2000)

Stratton, Roy Olin, *SACO, The Rice Paddy Navy* (Pleasantville, NY; C.S. Palmer Publishing, 1950)

Warner, Jeff, *US Naval Amphibious Forces* (Atglen, PA; Schiffer Publishing, 2007)

INDEX

References to images are in **bold**, references to plates are in **bold** with captions in (brackets).

Admiralty Islands 25
Adriatic Sea 8–9, **8**, **B1–2** (11)
Adriatic Special Operations Group 8–9, **B1–2** (11)
Andrews, Capt Charles 19
APDs 34, 36–37, **36**
Apexes 32–33
Aphis, HMS 20–21, **20**

balloons 16, **16**
Barb, USS 6
Bates, USS 48
beach defenses **D3** (27), **28**, **29**, **30**, 44, **44**
Beach Jumpers 13–21, **C** (15)
  clothing **B2** (11), **C** (15)
  operations 8–9, 18–21
  training 14, **C3** (15), **16**
  weapons and equipment **B2** (11), 14–18, **C** (15), **16**
Belknap, USS 45
Blessman, USS 48
boats
  Beach Jumpers 14–16, **16**
  Naval Group China 62
  NCDUs 25, 28, 30, 32–33
  Scouts & Raiders 4–5, **4**, 5, **10**
  UDTs 34, 36–38, **36**, **37**, **38**, 41, 42, 45
Borneo 26, 40, **F3** (47), 49
British COPP teams 6, 9
Burrfish, USS **E2** (39), 43–44
Burris-Meyer, Prof Harold 14, 18

Capaiuolo (U-Jäger 6071) 20–21
chaff 14, 18
Champe, Lt Joseph 56
Chiang Kai-shek 51
China *see* Naval Group China
clothing
  Beach Jumpers **B2** (11), **C** (15)
  Naval Group China 53, **G** (55), **H1–2** (59)
  NCDUs **D** (27)
  Scouts & Raiders **A** (7), **8**, **B1** (11)
  UDTs **F** (47)
coast-watching **G3** (55), 61–62, **61**

Dallas, USS 21–22
deception 14–21, **C** (15), **16**, **17**, **19**
demolition materials and explosives 23–24, **23**, **24**, **D** (27), 34, 35–36, **35**, **F2** (47), 49
Demonstration Group 80.4 18
Dickerson, USS 36
Diversion Task Group 4.0 19
Diversionary Task Group 77.11 21
diving equipment 26, 33–34, **E1** (39), **E3** (39), **F1** (49), **F3** (49)
Donovan, William 54

Elba 10, 16, 20
Emirau Island 25
Endicott, USS 13, 20, 21

Fairbanks, LtCdr Douglas, Jr 13–14, **13**, 19, 20–21
Fleet Radio Unit China 52, **52**
France, southern
  Beach Jumpers 10–12, **10**, **B3** (11), **C2** (15), **16**, 20–21
  NCDUs 31, 32–33

George Clymer, USS 22
Gilmer, USS 41
Goldsborough, USS 45

Green Island 25
Guam 42

Hagensen, Lt Carl P. 23–24
Hanlon, Capt B. Hall 44
"Happy Valley" 50, 51–52, **51**, 60–61
Harris, USS 6
Hewitt, Adm Henry K. 13–14, 19
Hopping, USS 48

Ie Shima **F2** (49)
Indochina, French 62
Italy **4**, **A2** (7), 8, **C1** (15), 19
Iwo Jima 46–48, **F1** (47)

Jaimeson, Lt Mitchell, drawings by **28**, **29**, **30**
Japan, US occupation 49, 50
Johnson, Capt Henry C. 20

Kauffman, LtCdr Draper 22–23, **22**, 44
Kemid Allah (U-Jäger 6083) 20–21
King, Adm Ernest 50, 53, 54
Kwajalein Atoll 38–40, **E1** (39)
Kweilin 52

LCC-60 9–10
LCI(D) 227 25
LCP(R)s 37–38, **37**, **38**, 41, 42, 45
LCR(L)s 38
Leedstown, USS 6
lights 4–5

Marianas 25
Marshall, Gen George C. 53
Marshalls 38–40
Mattmiller, John N. 58
Meynier, Robert and Katiou 62
Miles, Cdr Milton 50–51, **50**, 53–54, 56, 57, 61, 62
  pennant **H4** (59)
mines 56
Murray, Albert K., watercolours by **31**

Naval Combat Demolition Units (NCDUs) 21–33, **22**, **D** (27)
  clothing **D** (27)
  operations 25–33
  training 22–23
  weapons and equipment **B3** (11), 23–24, **23**, **24**, **25**, **26**, **D** (27), **28**, **30**
Naval Group China 50–62, **G** (55), **H** (59)
  clothing 53, **G** (55), **H1–2** (59)
  inter-service rivalries 53–54
  operations 56–62
  pennant **H4** (59)
  relations with USAAF 56
  training 51
  weapons and equipment **G1** (55), **H1** (59)
New Guinea 25–26, **D1** (27)
Noa, USS 25
Normandy 28
  NCDUs 23, **D2–3** (27), 28–32, **28**, **29**, **30**
  Scouts & Raiders **A2** (7), **A3** (7), 9–10
North Africa 5–6, **A1** (7), 21–2

Office of Strategic Services (OSS) 53–4
Okinawa 48–9
Orestes, USS 21

Pacific
  Beach Jumpers 21
  NCDUs 23, **24**, 25–26, **26**, **D1** (27)
  Scouts & Raiders 5, 12–13, **12**
  UDTs 33, **36**, **37**, 38–50, **E** (39), **F** (47)

Pact Doc hospital 60, **60**
Peleliu 5, **35**, **E2** (39), 43–44, **43**, **44**, **46**
Philippines 21, 26, 45
PT-201 8

radar jamming 16–18
Robinson, USS 43
rockets 14, **C2** (15), **16**

Saipan 41
Scarab, HMS 20–21
Scouts & Raiders 4–13, **A** (7)
  clothing **A** (7), **8**, **B1** (11)
  operations 5–13
  training 4
  weapons and equipment 4–5, **A2** (7), **10**, **B1** (11)
Seventh Amphibious Force 12–13, **12**, 25–26
Sicily 6, **A2** (7), 18, 22
smoke pots and smokescreens 14, **C3** (15), **16**
sonic deception and projectors 14, 16–18, **17**, **19**, **19**
Special Operations Task Group 80.4 20–21
Special Reconnaissance Detachment **E2** (39), 43–44
Steinbeck, John 19
Stilwell, Gen Joseph 53, 54
Stingrays 38–40
surfboards 37, 41
swim fins 34, **F1** (49), **F3** (49)

Tai Li, Gen 50–51, **50**, 53, 54, 56, 57, 58–60
Tarawa 33
Tatnall, USS 10–12
Tinian 43
training
  Beach Jumpers 14, **C3** (15), **16**
  of Chinese 50–51, **G1** (55), 56–60, **56**, **57**, **H1–2** (59)
  Naval Group China 51
  NCDUs 22–23
  Scouts & Raiders 4
  UDTs 38

Underwater Demolition Teams (UDTs) 33–50, **F** (47)
  clothing **F** (47)
  operations 12, 38–50
  training 38
  transportation 34, 36–38, **36**, **37**, **38**, 41, 42, 45
  weapons and equipment 33–36, **34**, **E3** (39), **F** (47)
US Army 4, 6, 53–54
USAAF 56

Vietnam 62
Vis 8, **8**, **B1–2** (11)

water depth, surveying 34–35
weapons and equipment
  Beach Jumpers **B2** (11), 14–18, **C** (15), **16**
  Naval Group China **G1** (55), **H1** (59)
  NCDUs **B3** (11), 23–24, **23**, **24**, **25**, **26**, **D** (27), **28**, **30**
  Scouts & Raiders 4–5, **A2** (7), **10**, **B1** (11)
  UDTs 33–36, **34**, **E3** (39), **F** (47)
weather observation **G2** (55), 60–61, **61**
Wedemeyer, Gen Albert 54

Yap **E2** (39), 43–44
Yugoslavia 8–9, **8**, **B1–2** (11)